RECORDKEEPING
THE SECRET TO GROWTH & PROFIT

by

LINDA PINSON
&
JERRY JINNETT

Published by

OUT OF YOUR MIND . . .
AND INTO THE MARKETPLACE™

Fullerton, CA 92633

RECORDKEEPING: The Secret to Growth and Profit

By Linda Pinson and Jerry Jinnett

First printing: April, 1988

Published by: OUT OF YOUR MIND....
              AND INTO THE MARKETPLACE™
              3031 Colt Way #223
              Fullerton, CA 92633

Cover design by Linda Pinson

Library of Congress Catalog Card No: 88-90667

ISBN 0-944205-14-3 (8½x11 paperbound)

Printed in the United States of America

Small Business Consulting
Textbooks
Seminars

**OTHER BUSINESS TEXTBOOKS
BY THESE AUTHORS:**

1.   **OUT OF YOUR MIND... AND INTO THE MARKETPLACE™**

2.   **ANATOMY OF A BUSINESS PLAN**

3.   **MARKETING:
RESEARCHING & REACHING YOUR TARGET MARKET**

For More Detailed Information:
PLEASE TURN TO THE LAST PAGE.

DEDICATION

This book is dedicated to Virginia Haverty, a wonderful friend who is now gone, but not forgotten. Her gifts of encouragement and confidence live on in the completion of our books.

ACKNOWLEDGEMENT

Many thanks go to Terry Peart of "Laserprint Publishing" without whose indomitable spirit this book could not have been completed by its almost impossible deadline.

Thanks, also, to our families who have put up with the many inconveniences caused by our single-mindedness while writing our books. With their encouragement and understanding, we have found it much easier to reach our goals.

This acknowledgement would not be complete without recognizing two more people who have improved the quality of this book. The first is Sue Area, who has donated her time to proofread all of our books. The second is Marilyn Dauber, C.P.A., whom we thank for her contribution of the last chapter of this book, entitled "Analyzing Financial Statements."

INTRODUCTION

Originally, we intended to title this book "2 + 2 = 5." The idea behind this title was that the end result of using records to evaluate trends and implement changes in your business can result in higher profits. Conversely, the failure to have an adequate recordkeeping system and to take advantage of the visibility it would provide to aid you in your business decisions can result in low profits--or no profits.

Two businesses having the same product, same number of sales, same unit cost of production, and the same unit sales price of their product can have a different end result. One company may take advantage of invoice discounts, evaluate production and decrease unit cost, keep a good Petty Cash Record to decrease reportable Net Income, and decrease theft through Inventory control. The competing company may do the opposite in each of these areas resulting in interest charges, no decreases in production costs, a false Net Income (resulting in more taxes) and a loss of Inventory due to theft.

Obviously, the first company would have increased their profits through good management (2 + 2 = 5), and the second company would have decreased profits because of poor business practices (2 + 2 = 3). Which all goes to prove that 2 + 2 may or may not =4.

It is the purpose of this book to help you to develop a basic understanding of business recordkeeping. Our ultimate goal would be to lead you step-by-step through the logical sequence of setting up your records and seeing the interrelationship of records, statements, and income tax accounting. We will then provide you with information to help you set up a general recordkeeping schedule. Our final chapter will be devoted to teaching you to analyze your records and thus be able to implement changes in your business that will result in increased profits.

In no way is this book intended to take the place of any kind of legal advice. It is merely a learning aid that we hope will prove to be of value to you. It has been a difficult task to organize this book, but if it proves to be effective in helping you to organize your recordkeeping system, then we will have accomplished our goal. Thank you for your confidence.

The Authors

TABLE OF CONTENTS

Small Business Consulting
Textbooks
Seminars

BASICS   ABOUT
RECORDKEEPING

1. BASICS ABOUT RECORDKEEPING

The keeping of accurate records is imperative if you are going to succeed at business. From time to time, we have had students in our small business classes who have wonderful ideas for products or services, but who do not want to be bothered with the details of recordkeeping. Their businesses are already doomed to failure.

FUNCTIONS OF RECORDKEEPING

The first is to provide you with information that will help you to see the trends that are taking place within your operation. You will see, as you study this book, that a complete and simple set of records will make it possible to tell at a glance what is happening with your business -- which areas are productive and cost-effective and which will require the implementation of changes. The second function of recordkeeping is to provide you with income tax information that can be easily retrieved and verified.

WHO SHOULD DO YOUR RECORDKEEPING

There is only one answer to this question. **YOU,** the business owner, must have a hands-on system, rather than delegating this job to an outsider. Keeping your own books and records will make you doubly aware of what is going on in your business. This is not meant to indicate the elimination of computer systems. "Hands-on" implies personal involvement in all recordkeeping whether it be hand-written or part of a business software package.

TYPES OF RECORDKEEPING

The system you use must be tailored to your individual needs. Obviously a service-oriented industry will not use the same records as a retail business. Because no two businesses will have exactly the same concerns, it is imperative that you develop your own system. You will have to consider any information that will be used by your particular venture and set up your records according to those needs.

WHEN DOES RECORDKEEPING BEGIN?

Your business commences as soon as you begin to refine your idea. You do not have to wait until you have a license and are open for business to start with your recordkeeping. In fact, you will do yourself a great disservice if you are not keeping records at this very moment. A good way to begin is as follows:

DIARY

Buy yourself a hardbound journal at your local stationers. Keep a diary of your thoughts and actions related to your new business. Number the pages, write in pen and initial any corrections you make. Your journal will serve to protect your idea as well as provide you with a record of your contacts and the information you gather for the future. You can also list any expenses incurred and file away your receipts. Be sure to date all entries.

BEGINNING JOURNAL

I like to utilize the last few pages of the journal to keep a record of Income and Expenses. It need not be complicated. You can set it up like the sample on Page 5.

SIMPLICITY IS THE KEY

At this point it is necessary to note that simplicity is the key to small business accounting. Your records must be complete, but not so complicated that they cannot be read and interpreted. It will be the function of this book to not only introduce you to the terminology and forms necessary to set up a recordkeeping system for your business, but to give you the understanding as to how you will be able to use those records to see trends and implement changes that will make your business venture more profitable and rewarding.

Note: Page 5 is an example of a Beginning Journal. On pages 6 and 7, you will find information on Common Deductible Expenses.

SAMPLE

BEGINNING JOURNAL

Date	Check No. (or Cash)	Paid To Whom	Income	Explanation of Debit or Credit	Credit	Debit

REMEMBER: All expenses relating to your new business endeavors should be recorded. A few examples are as follows:

1. Seminar and workshop fees

2. Mileage to and from business pursuits

3. Meals related to business (see Tax Rulings)

4. Written materials purchased for business

5. Office supplies (notebooks, journals, etc.)

6. Telephone calls relating to business

7. Professional organizations (dues, fees, etc.)

8. Materials used for developing product

9. Tools or equipment purchased for business

There are many other expenses which I have not mentioned. A good rule-of-thumb is that if a purchase or activity is related to business in any way, record it for future retrieval.

Note: Please read the text that follows this form for more information on deductions. There may be other expenses which apply to your business. Those listed below are the most common deductions.

DEDUCTIONS TO BE EXPENSED

ADVERTISING – yellow pages, newspaper, radio, direct mail, etc.
BAD DEBTS – from sales or services.
BANK SERVICE CHARGES – checks, etc.
BOOKS & PERIODICALS – bus.-related.
CAR & TRUCK EXPENSES – gas, repair, license, insurance, maintenance.
COMMISIONS – to sales reps.
CONTRACT SERVICES – independent.
CONVENTION EXPENSES
DISPLAY & EXHIBIT EXPENSES
DONATIONS
DUES – professional.
EDUCATIONAL FEES & MATERIALS
ELECTRIC BILLS
ENTERTAINMENT OF CLIENTS
FREIGHT – UPS, Postal, etc.
GAS BILLS
IMPROVEMENTS – under $100.00.
INSURANCE – business-related.
INTEREST PAID OUT
LAUNDRY & CLEANING – uniforms, etc.
LEGAL & PROFESSIONAL FEES
LICENSE FEE – business license.
MAINTENANCE – materials & labor.
OFFICE EQUIPMENT – under $100.00
OFFICE FURNITURE – under $100.00.
OFFICE SUPPLIES
PARKING FEES
PENSION & PROFIT-SHARING PLANS
POSTAGE
PRINTING EXPENSES
PROFESSIONAL SERVICES
PROMOTIONAL MATERIALS

PROPERTY TAX
PUBLICATIONS
REPAIRS
RUFUNDS, RETURNS & ALLOWANCES
SALES TAX – sales tax collected is Income. Reimbursement to SBE is deducted as an expense.
SALES TAX PAID – on purchases.
SUBSCRIPTIONS
TELEPHONE
TOOLS – used in trade and with a purchase price under $100.00.
UNIFORMS PURCHASED
UTILITIES – see gas, electric, and telephone.
WAGES PAID OUT

TO BE DEPRECIATED

BUSINESS PROPERTY
OFFICE FURNITURE – over $100.
OFFICE EQUIPMENT – over $100.
VEHICLES – used solely for business purposes.
TOOLS – purch. price over $100.
TANGIBLE PURCHASES – used for business and costing over $100. (not intended for resale)

The list of common tax-deductible expenses was prepared to help you identify many of those items which are **normally** deductible for income tax purposes. The new business owner should become familiar with those appropriate to the business. **DO NOT** wait until tax preparation time to look at this list. Knowing ahead of time which expenses are deductible will help you to better utilize them to your advantage while keeping proper records for income tax verification. **DO** keep in mind that this is only a partial list. There may very well be additional deductible expenses relating to your business. Call or visit the IRS. They have free publications and there are experts available to answer your questions. Another source of information is your accountant. Be sure to have documentation for all expenses so you can verify them if you are audited.

DEDUCTIBLE BUSINESS EXPENSES fall into two major categories: 1. Those which are deductible in their entirety in the year in which they are incurred, and 2. Those items considered depreciable, costing in excess of $100.00 and used in the operation of your business.

1. **Fully-deductible expenses** - All expenses incurred in the operation of your business are deductible and reduce your net income by their amount unless they are major expenses that fall in the depreciable category. These expenses will have to be itemized for tax purposes, and receipts should be easily retrievable for verification purposes.

2. **Depreciable expenses** - A rule of thumb is that those items costing in excess of $100.00 and used in connection with your business will be expensed through depreciation. Those assets generally include such things as office equipment, buildings, vehicles, etc. The Tax Reform 1987 contains strict rulings on depreciation. Information is available through the IRS. Depreciation is taken at a fixed rate and that portion allowed for the current year is deducted as an expense. It should be noted again that you **MAY NOT** use that item as both a fully-deductible expense and a depreciation expense. For example, a desk purchased for $500.00 in 1986 will have to be depreciated according to schedule at $100.00 per year for 5 years. If your total office equipment expense was $972.00, you must subtract the $500.00 leaving you with $472.00 fully-deductible expense for the year. The $100.00 depreciation for the desk is accounted for under depreciation expense. The additional $400.00 cost of the desk will be expensed equally to the next four years as depreciation.

HOME-BASED BUSINESSES - In order for your home to qualify as a business expense, that part of your home used in business pursuits must be used exclusively and on a regular basis in your work. For further information, you may dial the IRS Tele-Tax Information in your area or send for the free IRS Publication #587, "Business Use of Your Home".

2

INCOME
AND
EXPENSES

2. INCOME AND EXPENSES

All monies relating to your business fall under one of two classifications -- income or expense. It is necessary to understand some basic facts about each.

INCOME

Income is all the monies received by your business in any given period of time. It is made up of monies derived from retail sales, wholesale sales, sale of services, interest income and any miscellaneous income. You will want to be sure that you do not mix income with expenses. Under no circumstance do you use monies received to purchase goods and plan to deposit the remainder. A simple formula for tax accounting requires that your **income equals your deposits**. It is interesting to note that the IRS does not require you to keep copies of your receipt book if you follow this formula. The *income equals deposit equation* is supported by the 1986 Tax Reform.

EXPENSES

Expenses are all monies paid out by your business. They include those paid by check and those paid by cash. All require careful recording. Expenses fall into two distinct categories:

FIXED ASSETS OR CAPITAL
    a. The resources a business owns and does not intend for resale
        (land, buildings, equipment, etc.)
    b. These are Balance Sheet Accounts

OPERATING EXPENSES
    a. Direct and Indirect
    b. These are Income Statement Accounts

Before we proceed further, it is necessary for you to understand the difference between **Direct** and **Indirect** expenses.

DIRECT EXPENSES

These are expenses directly related to your product or service. This includes labor, materials, advertising and any product or service overhead (also known as variable or controllable).

INDIRECT EXPENSES

These are costs **not** directly related to your production or rendering of services. They include normal overhead (fixed expenses: office salaries, rents, licenses, office supplies, utilities, insurance, etc.). Indirect expenses are those which remain if your business suddenly ceases production or services for a period of time.

> **Note:** Some categories of expense may be divided into both direct and indirect. Examples are:
>
> ### Utilities
> Those used for production as differentiated from utilities consumed in the office, heating, restrooms, etc.
>
> ### Telephone
> Telemarketing and advertising are direct expenses. Monthly charges are indirect expenses.
>
> ### Freight and Postage
> Shipping of your product is a direct expense. Postage used as office overhead is an indirect expense.

Once you have a clear understanding of the above terms, you will be ready to proceed with the setting up of basic records from which information will be derived to formulate projected and performance statements of your business financial activity.

Small Business Consulting
Textbooks
Seminars

3

ESSENTIAL RECORDS
FOR
SMALL BUSINESS

3. ESSENTIAL RECORDS
FOR SMALL BUSINESS

Every small business will require certain records to keep track of its activities during the fiscal year. The most common are as follows:

1. General Journal
2. General Ledger
3. Petty Cash Record
4. Inventory Records
5. Depreciable Items Inventory
6. Accounts Receivable
7. Accounts Payable
8. Travel and Entertainment Record
9. Customer Records
10. Business Check Book
11. Filing System

Again, I would like to emphasize the need to keep your records as simple as possible. You will need to think about all the things that will pertain to your business and then determine the simplest way to have the information at your fingertips. I will discuss each of the above records, try to show you how they may be used, and finally give you an example of the form each can take. You will have to adapt these records to serve your particular business, eliminate any that are unnecessary and add new records to take care of areas not covered.

FORMAT

All of your records will be utilized in the development of your financial statements. The forms discussed in this section will provide you with records that are easy to use and interpret both by you and by anyone else who has occasion to retrieve information pertaining to your business.

FLOW OF ACCOUNTING DATA

After a transaction is completed, it must be recorded three times. The initial record of each transaction, or of a group of similar transactions, is evidenced by a business document such as a sales ticket, a check stub, or a cash register tape. On the basis of the evidence provided by that document, transactions are then entered in chronological order in the General Journal. The amounts of the debits and the credits in the journal are then transferred to the accounts in the ledger. The flow of data from transaction to ledger may be diagrammed as follows:

Business		Business		Entry recorded in		Entry posted to
TRANSACTION	<--->	DOCUMENT	<--->	JOURNAL	<-->	LEDGER
occurs		prepared				to individul accounts

DOUBLE ENTRY AND SINGLE ENTRY SYSTEMS

There are two basic bookkeeping methods.

SINGLE ENTRY

This is a term referring to a bookkeeping and accounting method which uses one set of books to record all transactions. This requires only a Journal which you maintain on a daily basis for recording receipts and expenditures, and a Ledger in which you or your accountant distribute expenditures and receipts under various accounts to indicate their purpose or source.

DOUBLE ENTRY

This is a bookkeeping and accounting method by which every transaction is recorded twice. This is based on the premise that every transaction has two sides. A sale, for example, is both a delivery of goods and a receipt of payment. On your Balance Sheet, the delivery of goods would be recorded as a credit (reduction of assets), while the payment would be counted as a debit (increase of assets). You should note that the words debit and credit do not have the usual connotation in this application. The two halves of the double entry always have to be equal. Many small businesses use only the single entry system, while larger businesses will need to set up their accounting by the double entry system. A clear understanding of the double entry system is necessary before using this method. A thorough study of it may be made from resources in your local library--or you may wish to have your accountant set it up for you.

GENERAL JOURNAL

A general journal is kept to record transactions made by your business. These transactions are recorded in the form of debits and credits.

1. **Debits** are all transactions for which monies are paid out.
2. **Credits** are the transactions for all monies received.

To make your accounting more effective, you will need to have enough columns in the general journal to cover major categories of expenses and income. If you have done your homework and figured out the areas of direct and indirect expenses, these divisions will serve as headings in your journal. Usually, a 12-column journal will suffice for most small businesses, but feel free to use more or less, as long as they are clear and easy to interpret.

It is suggested that you use a system of recordkeeping in the General Journal in which each entry is recorded twice -- once in the Credit or Debit Column and once in a corresponding individual column. For example, an advertising expense of $100 would be entered both in the Debit Column and under Advertising. When the columns are totaled, the amount under Debit will equal the sum of all expense columns. The Credit total will equal the sum of all income columns. This serves as a check for accuracy and will save hours of searching your records for errors when attempting to balance your books.

MISCELLANEOUS COLUMN

The last column in any General Journal should be Miscellaneous. This column serves as a catchall for any expense which does not fall under a main heading. For example, insurance may be paid only once a year and, therefore, a heading under that title would not be justified. Record that transaction first under Debit and secondly under Miscellaneous with an explanation either under the Transaction Column or in parenthesis next to the amount in the Miscellaneous Column. The explanation is a must, as you will want to categorize the expense in later statements and as tax information.

HEADINGS IN THE GENERAL JOURNAL

1. Check No.
2. Date
3. Transaction
4. Credit
5. Debit
6. Major Credit Headings
7. Major Debit Headings
8. Miscellaneous

TOTALS

Each column should be totaled at the bottom of each journal page. These totals are then transferred to the top of the next page and added in until you have completed a month. At the end of the month, the figures are transferred to a Profit and Loss Statement and a new month begins with a clean page and no balances.

A sample of a General Journal page with several transactions can be seen on page 20.

July 1987 - page 2

GENERAL JOURNAL
SAMPLE

CHECK #	DATE	TRANSACTION	CREDIT	DEBIT	SALES	S.TAX	REPAIRS	PURCH.	ADVERT.	MISCELL.
		Balance forward--	326 00	172 56	100 00	6 00	220 00	96 00	63 56	13 00
234	7/13	J.J. Advertising		32 00					32 00	
235	7/13	Rutger Products		51 00				51 00		
236	7/16	Regal Stationers		23 42						(off. supp.) 23 42
***	7/17	SALES Taylor	81 70		45 00	2 70				
		Jones			34 00 RESALE					
***	7/17	REPAIRS Davis $20, Jones $35, Smith $85	140 00				140 00			
237	7/19	PETTY CASH DEPOSIT		50 00						50 00
		TOTALS	547 70	328 98	179 00	8 70	360 00	113 00	95 56	120 42

GENERAL LEDGER

We have just seen how transactions are recorded in the Journal. The next step in the flow of accounting data is to transfer or post these same transactions to individual accounts in the General Ledger.

NUMBERING OF ACCOUNTS

In the next chapter of this book, we will be discussing Financial Statements. Two of these statements, the Balance Sheet and Income Statement are compiled from information derived from the accounts in the General Ledger.

Accounts in the General Ledger are divided into five major divisions:

1. **ASSETS**

2. **LIABILITIES**

3. **CAPITAL**

4. **REVENUE**

5. **EXPENSES**

Each division contains its own individual accounts which must be numbered. Although accounts in the ledger may be numbered consecutively as in the pages of a book, the flexible system of indexing is preferable.

To illustrate this concept, the following is a sample chart of accounts for a fictitious business. Each account has three digits. The first digit indicates the major division of the ledger in which the account is placed. Accounts beginning with (1) represent assets; (2) liabilities; (3) capital; (4) revenues; and (5) expenses. The second and third digits indicate the position of the account within its division. For example: In the chart below, Account Number 105 (Prepaid Rent), the **1** indiciates that Prepaid Rent is an asset account and the **5** indicates that it is in the fifth position within that division. A numbering system of this type has the advantage of permitting the later insertion of new accounts in their proper sequence without disturbing other account numbers. Using the three-digit system accomodates up to 99 separate accounts under each division. For a large enterprise with a number of departments or branches, it is not unusual for each account number to have four or more digits.

CHART OF ACCOUNTS
FOR A FICTITIOUS BUSINESS

Balance Sheet Accounts

1 Assets

101	Cash
102	Accounts
104	Supplies
105	Prepaid Rent
108	Production Equipment
109	Accumulated Depreciation

2. Liabilities

201	Accounts Payable
202	Salaries Payable

3. Capital

301	John Jones, Capital
302	Jone Jones, Capital
303	Income Summary

Income Statement Accounts

4 Revenue

401	Sales
405	Interest Income

5. Expenses

501	Rent Expense
504	Supplies Expense
505	Salary Expense
509	Depreciation Expense
514	Miscellaneous Expense

The best way for you to approach the setting up of your General Ledger is for you to make up a chart of the accounts you will use in your particular business, as illustrated above. You will then make a separate ledger page for each account. The ledger page should contain the account name and account number and individual columns for date, item, posting reference, debit, credit, and balance.

The following sample of a General Ledger page will illustrate the proper set-up for the posting of transactions from the journal to the ledger.

GENERAL LEDGER ACCOUNT

SAMPLE PAGE

	ACCOUNT Accounts Receivable				ACCOUNT NO. 101	

DATE	ITEM	POST. REF.	DEBIT	CREDIT	BALANCE DEBIT	CREDIT

NOTE: THE ACCOUNTS ARE NUMBERED IN ACCORDANCE WITH THE CHART OF ACCOUNTS. EACH ACCOUNT WOULD APPEAR ON A SEPARATE PAGE IN THE LEDGER.

PETTY CASH RECORD

Petty cash refers to all the small business purchases made with cash when it is not practical or convenient to pay by check. These purchases will add up swiftly and may account for several thousand dollars by the end of the year. Failure to account for them can result in a false picture of your business and additional cost in income taxes due. It is imperative that you keep an accurate record of all Petty Cash Expenditures, that you have receipts on file, and that you record them in a manner that will enable you to categorize these expenses under major headings at the end of an accounting period.

WHERE DO PETTY CASH FUNDS COME FROM?

In order to transfer cash into the Petty Cash Fund, you must first draw a check and debit it to Petty Cash in the General Journal (See sample in General Journal.) That same amount is credited in the Petty Cash Record as a deposit. When cash purchases are made, they are debited in the Petty Cash Record as Expenses. When the balance gets low, another check is drawn to rebuild the fund. After recording expenditures, file each receipt for easy retrieval should it become necessary.

PETTY CASH FORMAT

The two purposes of Petty Cash Accounting are: (1) To gather information that tells you where your money is being spent; and (2) For income tax retrieval. For both reasons, you will want as much information as possible on how much was spent and for what purpose. Any accountant will warn you that a large miscellaneous deduction will be suspect and may very well single your return out for an IRS audit. Therefore, I would like to suggest that you divide your Petty Cash Record into the following categories so that individual purchases may ultimately be debited to their appropriate expense accounts.

- a. Date of Transaction
- b. Purchased From Whom
- c. Expense Account to be debited
- d. Deposit
- e. Amount of Expense
- f. Balance in Fund

A sample Petty Cash Record is shown on the following page. Please Note: If you have purchased any items that need to be entered in other records (Ex: Inventory, Tools, etc.), do so when you debit Petty Cash. This will keep these records current and eliminate omitting them by mistake.

PETTY CASH RECORD

DATE	PURCHASED FROM	EXPENSE ACCT. DEBITED	DEPOSIT		EXPENSE		BALANCE	

Note: 1. Save all receipts for cash purchases!!!
       2. Record purchases WEEKLY in Petty Cash Record.
       3. File all receipts. These are deductible expenses.
       4. Be sure to record your Petty Cash deposits.

INVENTORY RECORD

The term **inventories** is used to designate: (1) Merchandise held for sale in the normal course of business; and (2) Materials in the process of production or held for such use. The recording of inventories is used both as an internal control and as a means of retrieval of information required for the computation of income tax.

THE GREAT INVENTORY MYTH

Before proceeding with the mechanics of keeping your inventory, I would like to clear up a misconception about the pros and cons of the relationship of inventory size and income tax due. Any business that has had to deal with inventory will almost certainly have heard the statement, "Put your cash into inventory. The larger it is, the few taxes you will have to pay." Conversely, you may also hear that if your inventory is reduced, your taxes will also be reduced. Both are nonsense statements, and I will prove it to you mathematically. The fact is that your net profit remains the same regardless of the amount reinvested in inventory. Ten thousand dollars is $10,000 in your checking account or on the shelves as saleable goods. This can be proved as follows:

Companies A & B: (1) both have a beginning inventory of $25,000
(2) both have gross sales of $30,000
(3) both sell their product at 100% markup and
thus reduce their beginning inventory by $15,000.

Company A: Reinvests $20,000 in inventory and deposits $10,000. This gives them an ending inventory of $30,000.

Company B: Reinvests $5,000 in inventory and deposits $25,000. The result is an ending inventory of $15,000.

The Net Profit is arrived at by subtracting your deductible expenses from your Gross Profit. We can prove that Companies A and B will in fact have the same Gross Profit and, therefore, the same Net Profit by using the following computation:

		Company A	Company B
1.	Beginning Inventory	$25,000	$25,000
2.	Purchase	$20,000	$ 5,000
3.	Add lines 1 & 2	$45,000	$30,000
4.	Less Ending Inventory	$30,000	$15,000
5.	Cost of Goods Sold (sub 4 from 3)	$15,000	$15,000
6.	Gross Receipts or Sales	$30,000	$30,000
7.	Less Cost of Goods Sold (line 5)	$15,000	$15,000
8.	Subtract line 7 from line 6		
	This is the **GROSS PROFIT**	**$15,000**	**$15,000**

It is very important that you understand the above concept. Inventory only affects your net profit as a vehicle to greater sales potential. How much or how little you stock at tax time will neither increase nor decrease your taxes. Companies A & B will both have a gross profit of $15,000, and will pay the same taxes.

INVENTORY CONTROL

Keeping records for the IRS is actually the lesser reason for keeping track of inventory. I personally know of two companies that nearly failed due to a lack of inventory control. One was a restaurant whose employees were carrying groceries out the back door at closing time. Although, the restaurant enjoyed a good clientele and followed sound business practices for the food industry, their year-end profit did not justify their existence. A careful examination of their records showed a failure to properly inventory their stock. By instituting strict inventory control, pilferage was ended and the next year's increase in profit saved the business. Inventory control in a retail business can help you to see such things as turnover time, high and low selling periods, changes in buying trends. Periodic examinations of your inventory and its general flow may be the meat of your existence.

BASIC INVENTORY RECORDS

Basic inventory records must contain the following information in order to be effective.

1. Date Purchased
2. Item Purchased (include stock no.)
3. Purchase Price (Cost)
4. Date Sold ⌐ (This information is especially helpful for determining
5. Sale Price ⌐ shelf life and trends in market value of your product.)

If your inventory is at all sizeable, you will want to program it into a computer. However, it is possible to keep it in hand-written form based on two premises: (1) You begin immediately; and (2) You keep it current and do it regularly. I have a clock shop with approximately two thousand items for sale. On any given day, I can show you I know how long I have had each item, which items are selling repeatedly and what time periods require the stocking of more inventory. Keep in mind that all businesses differ. Compile your inventory according to your specific needs. Be sure that it is divided in such a way as to provide quick reference. I sort mine out by using separate pages for each company from which I make my purchases. Another method might be to separate pages by type of item. The important thing is to make your inventory work for you.

THE MOST COMMON KINDS OF INVENTORIES ARE:

1. Merchandise or stock in trade
2. Raw materials
3. Work in process
4. Finished products
5. Supplies (that become a part of the item intended
    for sale)

To arrive at a dollar amount for your inventory, you will need a method for **identifying** and a basis for **valuing** the items in your inventory. Inventory valuation must clearly show income and, for that reason, you must use this same inventory practice from year to year.

In some businesses, there is specific identification of items with their costs and there is no question as to which items remain in the inventory. In those businesses dealing with a large quantity of like items, there must be a method for deciding which items were sold and which remain in inventory. The two methods are as follows:

1. FIFO (first-in-first-out) - assumes that the items you purchased or produced first are the first sold.

2. LIFO (last-in-first-out) - assumes that the items of inventory that you purchased or produced last are sold first. You must check tax rules to qualify before electing this method.

For a new business using FIFO, you may use either the cost method or the lower of cost or market method to value your inventory. You must use the same method to value your entire inventory, and you **may not** change to another method without the permission of the IRS.

The two pages that follow are samples of Inventories. The first is for specific identification of items -- those products which differ from each other and can be identified by stock number and description. These are the items that can be individually accounted for as to purchase date, cost, sale date and sale price. The second sample is for non-identifiable goods. An example would be the purchase or production of 2,000 units of a like item -- the first thousand being produced at a unit cost of $5.00 and the second at a unit cost of $6.00. It would be impossible to determine which remain in inventory and these must be identified by the FIFO or LIFO method and valued accordingly to figure taxable income.

For further information on inventory rules, please read Chapter 8 in the IRS Publication 334 (Rev. Nov. 87) *Tax Guide for Small Business*.

Recordkeeping: The Secret to Growth and Profit

INVENTORY RECORD

(IDENTIFIABLE ITEMS)

DATE PURCH.	INVENTORY PURCHASED (description & stock no.)	PURCH. PRICE	BUYER'S NAME	SALE DATE	SALE PRICE	SALES TAX

NOTE: The Inventory Record shown here is to be used for keeping track of goods purchased for resale. Each page should deal with only one type of item or with goods purchased from one wholesaler. Use that company's name as a heading. If you buy like items from several sources, use the type of purchase as a heading. This will make the information easy to retrieve when it is needed. Inventories for your own tools, equipment, etc. do not need the last four columns.

KEEP YOUR INVENTORY CURRENT!!!

INVENTORY RECORD
(NON-IDENTIFIABLE ITEMS)

PRODUCTION OR PURCHASE DATE	DESCRIPTION OF ITEM	NUMBER OF UNITS	UNIT COST	MARKET VALUE ON DATE OF INVENTORY

Note: These items are inventoried by a physical count or by computer records. They are then valued according to rules that apply for FIFO or LIFO. Read the information in your tax guide carefully before determining inventory value.

Recordkeeping: The Secret to Growth and Profit

FIXED ASSETS LOG

At the end of each tax year you will have to provide your accountant with a list of all assets that have been capitalized. These are items purchased for use in your business at a cost in excess of $100 and not debited to a "500" or Expense Account. An example might be an electronic typewriter costing $700 which could either be depreciated or expensed entirely in the year of purchase.

It is a good idea to keep a running inventory of depreciable purchases along with the following information:

(1) Asset Purchased
(2) Purchase Price
(3) Purchase Date
(4) Number Years to be Depreciated
(5) Date Sold
(6) Sale Price

Depreciation can be very tricky and the laws change from time to time. Your job is to be able to provide your accountant with basic information. His is to apply the law to maximize your benefits. With the following form, you can do your part and have a general overview of what assets you have that fall in this category. Be aware that you are also accountable for disposition of these items. If you have depreciated an automobile down to $2,000 and then sell it for $3,500, you will have to report a profit of $1,500.

A sample of Fixed Assets Log can be found on Pages 32.

FIXED ASSETS LOG

ASSSETS PURCHASED	PURCH. DATE	PURCH. PRICE	DEPREC. ALLOWED	NO. YRS. TO BE DEPREC.	DATE SOLD	SALE PRICE

Note: See IRS Pub. 334 (Rev. Nov. 87) "Tax Guide for Small Business", (Chapter 12) for more detailed information on depreciation.

ACCOUNTS RECEIVABLE

This ledger is used to keep track of money owned to your business as a result of sale of a product or the rendering of services. You will need to set up your records with the following information:

    (1)   Name of Account
    (2)   Account Number
    (3)   Invoice Date
    (4)   Invoice Number
    (5)   Invoice Amount
    (6)   Terms of Invoice (Ex: 2% net 10)
    (7)   Amount Paid
    (8)   Date Paid
    (9)   Balance

Each client with an open account should have a separate page with account information.

At the end of a predetermined billing period, each account will be sent a statement showing their invoice number and amounts and the balance due. The statement should also include terms of payment. When the payment is received, it is recorded on the accounts receivable record. The total of all the outstanding balances in Accounts Receivable is transferred to Current Assets when preparing a Balance Sheet for your business.

An example of an Accounts Receivable form follows this page 34.

ACCOUNTS PAYABLE

Those debts owed by your company for goods purchased or services rendered to you in the pursuit of your business. If you are going to have a good credit record, the payment of these invoices must be timely and you will need an efficient system for keeping track of what you owe and when it should be paid. **When your accounts payable are not numerous** and you do not accumulate unpaid invoices by partial payments, you may wish to use an accordion file divided into the days of the month. Invoices Payable may be directly filed under the date on which they should be paid, taking into account discounts available for early payment.

If your Accounts Payable are stretched over a longer period, you will need to keep separate records for the creditors with whom you do business. You will most certainly be billed regularly for the balance of your account, but the individual records will help you to see what is happening in this area. They should be reviewed monthly and an attempt should be made to satisfy all your creditors. When preparing the Balance Sheet, the total for Accounts Payable should be transferred to the Current Liabilities portion of that statement.

A sample form for Accounts Payable can be seen on the next page .

SAMPLE
ACCOUNTS RECEIVABLE

NAME OF CUSTOMER_____

ACCOUNT NO._____

INVOICE DATE	INVOICE NO.	INVOICE AMOUNT	TERMS	DATE PAID	AMOUNT PAID	BALANCE

Recordkeeping: The Secret to Growth and Profit

SAMPLE
ACCOUNTS PAYABLE

NAME OF CREDITOR _____

ACCOUNT NO. _____

INVOICE DATE	INVOICE NO.	AMOUNT OF INVOICE		DATE PAID	AMOUNT PAID		BALANCE DUE	

TRAVEL AND ENTERTAINMENT

You will have to prove your deductions for travel, transportation, and entertainment business expenses by adequate records or by sufficient evidence that will support your claim. **Records required** should be kept in an account book, diary, statement of expense, or similar record. In the following paragraphs, we will discuss general information pertaining to transportation expenses, meal and entertainment expenses, and travel expenses. It is import that these expenses be recorded as they occur. It is difficult to remember them accurately after the fact.

TRANSPORTATION EXPENSES

These are the ordinary and necessary expenses of getting from one work place to another in the course of your business (when you are not traveling away from home).

Car Expenses

If your car is used solely for business purposes, you may be able to take a deduction for car expenses (i.e., gas, oil, tires, repairs, insurance, depreciation, interest, taxes, license, garage rent, parking fees, etc). If the use of the car is for both business and personal use, you must divide your expenses and deduct the percentage used in business pursuit. **The standard mileage rate** may be used instead of figuring actual expenses. This requires a log recording the business miles traveled during the year.

MEALS AND ENTERTAINMENT EXPENSES

These are deductible only if they are ordinary and necessary expenses of carrying on your trade or business and can be provided by using current tax rules of reporting.

You must be able to show that they are:

1. **Directly related** to the active conduct of your trade or business, or
2. **Associated** with the active conduct of your trade or business.

Beginning in 1987, you may deduct only 80% of business-related meals and entertainment expenses. You must record these expenses with date, location, reason, client information, amount paid, who was present from your business, and a receipt for the expense.

TRAVEL EXPENSES

These are deductible while away from home if you can prove:

1. Each separate amount you spent.
2. Dates you left and returned home and number of days spent on business away from home.
3. Destination of travel by name or description.
4. Business reason or benefit expected to gain from travel.

These expenses include transportation, lodging, meals, and related items.

The next three pages are samples of:

(1) Mileage Log
(2) Entertainment Expense Record
(3) Travel Record

For more detailed information, see Chapter 15, IR's Publication 334 (Rev. Nov. 87) *Tax Guide for Small Business.*

MILEAGE LOG

DATES: From_____ To_____

DATE	LOCATION		REASON FOR TRIP	NUMBER OF MILES
	FROM	TO		

NOTE: 1. Mileage records are required by the IRS if you do not use your vehicle 100% for business purposes and claim a mileage deduction.

2. Keep your log in your vehicle and record your mileage as it occurs. It is very difficult to recall after the fact.

ENTERTAINMENT EXPENSE RECORD

DATES: From_____ To_____

DATE	LOCATION	BUSINESS REASON	CLIENT INFORMATION	BUSINESS REP. PRESENT	COST	

NOTE: 1. For more information on Meals or Entertainment, please refer to IRS Publication 463, "Travel, Entertainment, and Gift Expenses".

TRAVEL RECORD

TRIP TO: _____

REASON: _____

DATES: From _____ To _____

DATE	TIME	LOCATION	REASON FOR EXPENSE	COST	

NOTE: 1. You must prove each separate amount you spent for travel away from home, such as the cost of your transportation or lodging.

2. You may total the daily cost of your meals and other incidental elements of such travel if they are listed in reasonable categories, such as meals, gas and oil, and taxi fares.

3. For more information, see IRS Publication 463.

CUSTOMER INFORMATION RECORDS

These records are kept as a means of helping a business deal more effectively with its customers. This is especially true in the service industry and in small businesses dealing in specialty retail sales. Many other types of business have no way to keep specialized information on customers due to volume or change in clientele. However, if you can incorporate such records into your operation, you will find that they will greatly enhance your credibility with your customers. Service businesses generally strive for repeat and referral business plus new customers who come to them through commercial advertising. Specialty retail sales shops also look for repeats and referrals as their primary source of business. By keeping a file of 3"x5" index cards -- one on each customer -- the business owner can have a wealth of ready information at his fingertips. The types of things that can be recorded and some uses of that information are as follows:

SERVICE INDUSTRY

Includes:
Name, address, telephone numbers (work and home), service performed, charges, special advice to customer, guarantees given, any information you may feel to be helpful.

Some uses of Information:
Protection of the Business from Customers' claims that services were performed which were not recorded, information as proof of dates of warranty service (benefitting both customer and business owner), information to help business owners remember a customer, give that customer specialized attention.

SPECIALTY RETAIL SALES BUSINESS

Includes:
Name, address, telephone numbers (work and home), sales information, special interests of customer.

Some uses of Information:
Use as a mailing list for special sales; when customer calls, use card to jog your memory as to his interests, what he has already purchased and what he might like. These customers like to be remembered and have personalized attention.

If you have the time and capability to keep customer file cards, you will greatly enhance your business. On the next page you will find samples of customer files for: (1) The Service Industry; and (2) Specialty Retail Sales.

SAMPLE CUSTOMER FILES

1. SERVICE INDUSTRY

```
Jones, John W.                    (H) (714) 726-4289
123 W. 1st St.
Anywhere, CA  97134               (W) (713) 853-1234


1. Ridgeway G/F Clock (IHS)    a. Repaired pendulum, rep.
        $55.00    8/19/82          susp. sprg., serviced.

2. S/Thomas O.G.    a. Cleaned, bushed movement, balanced.
        $155.00   6/07/85         Guarantee: 1 year

3. Waltham L/W/W (antique)    a. Stem, clean, repair hspg.
        $45.00    7/11/87
```

2. SPECIALTY RETAIL SALES

```
Smith, Henry L.  (D.D.S.)          (W) (201) 625-1304
76 Main Street
Somewhere, CA  96072

*Buys for wife's (Ann) collection      Birthday, May 3rd
                                       Anniversary, Oct. 21st

1. O8 CM  M/Box w/"Lara's Theme"  1/18  (Rosewood burl)
        $42.00 + Tax     4/28/87

2. 789 BMP  3/72 w/"18th Variation"  $625.00 + Tax  10/17/87

3. Novelty - Bear w/Heart    $32.00+ Tax    2/13/88
```

RECEIPT FILES

WHERE DO YOU KEEP RECEIPTS?

It is required by the IRS that you be able to verify deductions. For that reason alone, you must have a filing system that makes receipts easy to retrieve. For most small businesses an accordion file divided into alphabet pockets will be the most efficient way of filing your receipts. You may wish to keep a separate file for Petty Cash Receipts. I use the same one for those paid by check and by cash. At the end of the year, I add my bank statements, journal, a copy of my tax return, and any other pertinent information for that year. All are put away in the one accordion file and labeled with the year. If, at a later date, I need information for a tax audit or for another purpose, everything is in one place.

This is the last of the Basic Records to be discussed. In the next section of this book we will consider Financial Statements and how they are developed from the records with which we have just been concerned.

INTRODUCTION TO
FINANCIAL STATEMENTS

4. INTRODUCTION TO FINANCIAL STATEMENTS

In the previous chapters of this book, we have introduced you to the functions and types of recordkeeping, some simple accounting terminology, and the essential records to be used in small business. Now it is time to see how statements are developed from your records and how the use of those financial statements can help you to see the financial condition of your business and to identify its relative strengths and weaknesses. The business owner who takes the time to understand and evaluate his operation through financial statements over the life of the business will be far ahead of the entrepreneur who concerns himself only with his product or service. Financial statements fall into two main categories: (1) **Actual Performance Statements**; and (2) **Pro Forma Statements.**

Performance statements record the past performance of your business and are a written summary of its financial activities. Pro forma statements are forecasts portraying a realistic measurement of future financial activity. Both are important to your understanding the financial health of your business -- and to enable you to plan for business growth.

Financial statements will be presented in the following order:

Actual Performance Statements
   a. Balance Sheet
   b. Profit and Loss Statement (or Income Statement)
   c. Business Financial History (composite of a., b., and legal structure
         information)
Pro Forma Statements
   a. Pro Forma Cash Flow Statement (or Budget)
   b. Quarterly Budget Analysis (means of evaluating projected with
      actual performance within budget)
   c. Three - Five Year Projection (Pro Forma Income Statement)
   d. Break-Even Analysis

Each of the above financial statements will be discussed as to (1) definition and use, (2) how to develop the statement, and (3) information sources. The text for each will be followed by a sample statement.

BALANCE SHEET

The Balance Sheet is a financial statement that shows the condition of the business as of a fixed date. It is usually done at the close of an accounting period. The Balance Sheet can be compared to a photograph. It is a picture of your firm's financial condition at a given moment and will show you whether your financial position is strong or weak. By regularly preparing this statement, you will be able to identify and analyze trends in the financial strength of your business and thus implement timely modifications.

HOW TO DEVELOP A BALANCE SHEET

All Balance Sheets contain three categories - Assets, Liabilities, and Net Worth. The three are related in that at any given time, a business's assets equal the total contributions by its creditors and owners. This is simply illustrated in the following formula:

ASSETS   =   LIABILITIES   +   NET WORTH

(anything your business   (Debts owed by the busi-   (An amount equal to
owns that has monetary value)   ness to any of its creditors)   the owner's equity)

> **Note:** With the application of simple mathematical principles, the formula may also be written as follows:

ASSETS   —   LIABILITIES   =   NET WORTH

It then becomes apparent that if a business possesses more assets than it owes to creditors, its net worth will be a positive. Conversely, if the business owes more than it possesses in assets, the net worth will be a negative.

The Balance Sheet must follow an accepted format and contain the above-mentioned categories. They have been established by a system know as GAAP (General Accepted Accounting Principles). By doing so, anyone reading the Balance Sheet can readily interpret it.

INFORMATION FOR THE BALANCE SHEET

The Balance Sheet is drawn up by using the totals from individual accounts discussed in the previous section. The accounts numbered 100-199 are Assets. The accounts numbered 200-299 are Liabilities. The accounts numbered 300-399 are Net Worth on capital accounts. In other words Asset figures are derived from Bank Statements, Petty Cash, Accounts Receivable, Inventory, Accounts Depreciable and any appropriate General Ledger totals. Liabilities are derived from Accounts Payable, Notes Payable, Estimated Tax computations, Employee Contracts and Sales Tax Collected. The Net Worth figures represent totals invested by each of the owners plus any profits or minus any losses that have accumulated in the business. The next two pages contain: (1) Explanation of Balance Sheet Categories; and (2) Sample Balance Sheet.

BALANCE SHEET

(Explanation of Categories on Balance Sheet)

I. ASSETS - Everything owned by or owed to the business that has cash value

A. Current Assets - Assets that can be converted into cash within one year of the date on the Balance Sheet

    1. Cash - Money you have on hand. Include monies not yet deposited.
    2. Petty Cash - Money deposited to Petty Cash & not yet expended.
    3. Accounts Receivable - Money owed to you for goods and/or services
    4. Inventory - Raw materials, work in process and goods manufactured or purchased for resale.
    5. Short-Term Investments - (Expected to be converted to cash within one year) Stocks, bonds, C.D.'s. List at the lesser of cost or market value.
    6. Prepaid Expenses - Goods/services purchased or rented prior to use.

B. Long-Term Investments - Stocks, bonds, and special savings accounts to be kept for at least one year.

C. Fixed Assets - The resources a business owns and does not intend for resale.

    1. Land - List at original purchase price.
    2. Buildings - List at cost less depreciation.
    3. Equipment, Furniture, Autos/Vehicles - List at cost less depreciation. Kelley Blue Book can be used to determine value of autos/vehicles.

D. Other Assets - Any assets not listed above. List separately and value in terms of current worth.

II. LIABILITIES - What your business owes; claims by creditors on your assets.

A. Current Liabilities - Obligations payable within one operating cycle

    1. Accounts Payable - Amounts owed by you for goods or services.
    2. Notes Payable - Short-term notes, list the balance of principal due. Separately list the current portion of long-term notes.
    3. Interest Payable- Interest accrued on loans and credit.
    4. Taxes Payable - Amounts estimated to have been incurred during accounting period.
    5. Payroll Accrual - Current Liabilities on salaries and wages.

B. Long-Term Liabilities - Outstanding balance less current portion due. (Ex. - Mortgage)

III. NET WORTH - Also called "EQUITY" - The claims of the owner or owners on the assets of the business.

A. Proprietorship or Partnership - each owner's original investment plus earnings after withdrawals.
B. Corporation - The sum or contributions by owners or stockholders plus earnings retained after paying dividends.

Company Name

B A L A N C E   S H E E T

_____ ____, 19____

ASSETS		LIABILITIES	
		Current Liabilities	
		Accounts Payable	$_____
Current Assets		Notes Payable	$_____
Cash	$_____	Interest Payable	$_____
Petty Cash	$_____	Taxes Payable	
Accounts Receivable	$_____	Fed. Inc. Tax	$_____
Inventory	$_____	State Inc. Tax	$_____
Short-Term Investments	$_____	Self-Emp. Tax	$_____
Prepaid Expenses	$_____	Sales Tax (SBE)	$_____
		Property Tax	$_____
		Payroll Accrual	$_____
Long-Term Investments	$_____	**Long-Term Liabilities**	
		Notes Payable	$_____
Fixed Assets			
Land	$_____	**TOTAL LIABILITIES**	$_____
Buildings	$_____		
Improvements	$_____	**NET WORTH**	
Equipment	$_____	Proprietorship	$_____
Furniture	$_____	or	
Autos/Vehicles	$_____	Partnership	
		(Name's) Equity	$_____
		(Name's) Equity	$_____
		or	
Other Assets		Corporation	
1.	$_____	Capital Stock	$_____
2.	$_____	Surplus Paid In	$_____
3.	$_____	Retained Earnings	$_____
4.	$_____	**TOTAL NET WORTH** $_____	
		Assets — Liabilities = Net Worth	
TOTAL ASSETS	$_____	Total Liabilities and Equity will <u>always</u> be equal to Total Assets!	

PROFIT AND LOSS STATEMENT
(ALSO KNOWN AS: INCOME STATEMENT)

The Profit and Loss Statement shows your business financial activity over a specific period of time. It must be prepared not only at the end of the fiscal year, but at the close of each business month. In contrast to the Balance Sheet, which shows a picture of your business at a particular moment, the Profit and Loss Statement can be likened to a moving picture -- showing where your money came from and where it was spent over a specific period of time. It is an excellent tool for assessing what is happening in your business. You will be able to pick out weaknesses in your operation and plan ways to run your business more effectively and thereby increase your profits. For example, you may discover that a heavy advertising expenditure in March did not result in a higher sales volume in the following period. Next year, you may decide to utilize your advertising funds more effectively by spending them at a time when you anticipate a period of increased customer spending. Also, you might examine your Profit and Loss Statement for periods of high sales volume and plan your future inventory accordingly. Comparison of Profit and Loss Statements from several years will give you an even better picture of the trends in your business. Do not underestimate the value of this tool.

HOW TO DEVELOP A PROFIT AND LOSS STATEMENT

The Profit and Loss Statement must also follow an accepted format according to GAAP and contain the following categories in a particular order:

INCOME
1. Net Sales (Gross sales less returns and allowances)
2. Cost of Goods Sold (See Form 1040, Schedule C for computation)
3. Gross Profit (Net sales minus cost of sales)

EXPENSES
1. Selling Expenses (Direct Expenses)
2. Administrative Expenses (Indirect Expenses)

TOTAL EXPENSES

INCOME FROM OPERATIONS (Income minus Expenses)

OTHER INCOME (such as Interest Income)

NET PROFIT (LOSS) BEFORE INCOME TAXES

INCOME TAXES

NET PROFIT (after Taxes)

INFORMATION SOURCE FOR PROFIT AND LOSS STATEMENT

At the end of each month, the accounts in the General Ledger are balanced and closed. Income and Expense account balances are used in the Profit and Loss Statement, these are the Revenue Accounts numbered 400-499 and the Expense Accounts number 500-599. We have enclosed two forms for your use. The first is divided into twelve months. Fill it in monthly after balancing your ledger. At the end of the year, this form will provide an accurate picture of your financial activity. The second form can be used for your monthly and annual Profit and Loss or Income Statements. See pages 53 and 54.

PROFIT AND LOSS STATEMENT

FOR THE YEAR 19_____.

	JAN	FEB	MAR	APR	MAY	JUN	JUL	AUG	SEP	OCT	NOV	DEC
INCOME												
1. Net Sales												
2. Cost of Goods Sold												
3. Gross Profit on Sales												
EXPENSES												
1. Selling Expense (Direct)												
a. ADVERTISING												
b. FREIGHT												
c. PACKAGING COSTS												
d. PARTS & SUPPLIES												
e. SALES SALARIES												
f. MISC. DIRECT EXP.												
2. Admin. Exp. (Indirect)												
a. DEPRECIATION EXPENSE												
b. INSURANCE												
c. LICENSES & PERMITS												
d. OFFICE SALARIES												
e. RENT EXPENSE												
f. UTILITIES												
g. MISCELL. INDIR. EXP.												
TOTAL EXPENSES												
INCOME FROM OPERATIONS												
OTHER INCOME (Interest)												
OTHER EXPENSE (Interest)												
INCOME BEFORE TAXES												
INCOME TAXES												
NET INCOME												

INCOME STATEMENT

(Also Called: Profit & Loss Statement)

For the Period Beginning_____and Ending_____.

INCOME

    1. NET SALES (Gross - Ret. & Allow.)

    2. Cost of Goods Sold
        a. Inventory (January 1st)
        b. Purchases
        c. Cost of goods avail. for sale (a.+b.)
        d. Deduct Inventory December 31st

    3. GROSS PROFIT ON SALES

EXPENSES

    1. Selling Expense (Direct or Controllable)
        a. Advertising
        b. Freight
        c. Legal Fees
        d. Packaging Costs
        e. Parts & Supplies
        f. Sales Salaries
        g. Miscellaneous Direct Expenses

    2. Administrative Expense (Indirect, Fixed)
        a. Depreciation Expense
        b. Insurance
        c. Licenses & Permits
        d. Office Salaries
        e. Rent Expense
        f. Taxes & Licenses
        g. Utilities
        h. Miscellaneous Indirect Expenses

    TOTAL EXPENSES

INCOME FROM OPERATIONS (Inc. less Exp.)

OTHER INCOME
    1. Interest Income

OTHER EXPENSE
    1. Interest Expense

NET PROFIT (LOSS) BEFORE INCOME TAXES

INCOME TAXES

NET PROFIT (LOSS) AFTER INCOME TAXES

BUSINESS FINANCIAL HISTORY

The Business Financial History is a summary of financial information about your company from its start to the present. It is the last of the statements required by all potential lenders. If you are a new business, the lending institution will require a personal financial history of each owner. This statement is a composite of information contained in your other statements plus information on its legal structure.

HOW TO DEVELOP A FINANCIAL HISTORY

Financial Statements are generally divided into the following areas:

a. Assets
b. Liabilities
c. Net Worth
d. Contingent Liabilities
e. Inventory Details
f. Profit and Loss Statement
g. Real Estate Holdings
h. Stocks and Bonds

i. Sole Proprietorship Info
   Schedule C
j. Partnership Information
   Schedule D
k. Corporation Information
   Schedule E
l. Schedule F
m. Insurance Coverage

INFORMATION SOURCES OF FINANCIAL HISTORY

a. Assets, Liabilities, Net Worth, and Contingent Liabilities (figures are derived from your Balance Sheet)
b. Inventory Details are arrived at from your Inventory Record and current policies.
c. Profit and Loss Statement information is transferred from your yearly Profit and Loss Statement or the combination of several, if required by the lender.
d. Real Estate Holdings and Stocks and Bonds information will take a little effort on your part. You will have to sort through papers pertaining to each.
e. Sole Proprietorship, Partnership or Corporation sections are filled out according to your particular legal structure.
f. Schedule F must be filled out and lists information on your particular business history.
g. Insurance Coverage details information on the amounts of individual coverage and beneficiary.

Note: Samples of Business and Personal Financial Statements follow on pages 56 through 59.

SAMPLE FINANCIAL STATEMENT
(Business)

FINANCIAL STATEMENT
INDIVIDUAL, PARTNERSHIP, OR CORPORATION

FINANCIAL STATEMENT OF

NAME _____

ADDRESS _____

RECEIVED AT _____ BRANCH

BUSINESS _____

AT CLOSE OF BUSINESS _____ 19___

To

The undersigned, for the purpose of procuring and establishing credit from time to time with you and to induce you to permit the undersigned to become indebted to you on notes, endorsements, guarantees, overdrafts or otherwise, furnishes the following (or in lieu thereof the attached, which is the most recent statement prepared by or for the undersigned) as being a full, true and correct statement of the financial condition of the undersigned on the date indicated, and agrees to notify you immediately of the extent and character of any material change in said financial condition, and also agrees that if the undersigned, or any endorser or guarantor of any of the obligations of the undersigned, at any time fails in business or becomes insolvent, or commits an act of bankruptcy, or if any deposit account of the undersigned with you, or any other property of the undersigned held by you, be attempted to be obtained or held by writ of execution, garnishment, attachment or other legal process, or if any of the representations made below prove to be untrue, or if the undersigned fails to notify you of any material change as above agreed, or if the business, or any interest therein, of the undersigned is sold, then and in such case, at your option, all of the obligations of the undersigned to you, or held by you, shall immediately become due and payable, without demand or notice. This statement shall be construed by you to be a continuing statement of the condition of the undersigned, and a new and original statement of all assets and liabilities upon each and every transaction in and by which the undersigned hereafter becomes indebted to you, until the undersigned advises in writing to the contrary.

ASSETS	DOLLARS	CENTS	LIABILITIES	DOLLARS	CENTS
Cash In _____ **(NAME OF BANK)**			Notes Payable to Banks _____		
Cash on Hand _____			Notes Payable and Trade Acceptances for Merchandise _____		
Notes Receivable and Trade Acceptance (Includes $_____ Past Due) _____			Notes Payable to Others _____		
Accounts Receivable—$_____ Less Reserves $_____			Accounts Payable (Includes $_____ Past Due) _____		
Customer's . . . (Includes $_____ Past Due)			Due to Partners, Employes, Relatives, Officers, Stockholders or Allied Companies		
Merchandise—Finished—How Valued _____			Chattel Mortgages and Contracts Payable (Describe Monthly Payments) . . . $_____		
Merchandise—Unfinished—How Valued _____			Federal and State Income Tax _____		
Merchandise—Raw Material—How Valued _____			Accrued Liabilities (Interest, Wages, Taxes, Etc.) _____		
Supplies on Hand _____			Portion of Long Term Debt Due Within One Year _____		
Stocks and Bonds—Listed (See Schedule B) _____					
TOTAL CURRENT ASSETS			**TOTAL CURRENT LIABILITIES**		
Real Estate—Less Depreciation of: $_____ Net (See Schedule A)			Liens on Real Estate (See Schedule A) $_____		
Machinery and Fixtures— Less Depreciation of: $_____ Net			Less Current Portion Included Above $_____ Net		
Automobiles and Trucks— Less Depreciation of: $_____ Net					
Stocks and Bonds—Unlisted (See Schedule B) _____			Capital Stock—Preferred _____		
Due from Partners, Employes, Relatives, Officers, Stockholders or Allied Companies _____			Capital Stock—Common _____		
			Surplus—Paid In _____		
Cash Value Life Insurance _____			Surplus—Earned and Undivided Profits _____		
Other Assets (Describe) _____			Net Worth (If Not Incorporated) _____		
TOTAL			**TOTAL**		

PROFIT AND LOSS STATEMENT FOR THE PERIOD FROM _____ TO _____

			CONTINGENT LIABILITIES (NOT INCLUDED ABOVE)		
Net Sales (After Returned Sales and Allowances) _____			As Guarantor or Endorser _____		
Cost of Sales:			Accounts, Notes, or Trade Acceptances Discounted or Pledged _____		
Beginning Inventory			Surety On Bonds or Other Continent Liability _____		
Purchases (or cost of goods mfd.)			Letters of Credit _____		
TOTAL			Judgments Unsatisfied or Suits Pending _____		
Less: Closing Inventory			Merchandise Commitments and Unfinished Contracts _____		
Gross Profit on Sales			Merchandise Held On Consignment From Others _____		
			Unsatisfied Tax Liens or Notices From the Federal or State Governments of Intention to Assess Such Liens _____		
Operating Expenses:			**RECONCILEMENT OF NET WORTH OR EARNED SURPLUS**		
Salaries—Officers or Partners					
Salaries and Wages—Other			Net Worth or Earned Surplus at Beginning of Period _____		
Rent			Add Net Profit or Deduct Net Loss _____		
Depreciation			Total _____		
Bad Debts			Other Additions (Describe) _____		
Advertising			Total _____		
Interest			Less: Withdrawals or Dividends _____		
Taxes—Other Than Income			Other Deductions (Explain) _____		
Insurance			Total Deductions _____		
Other Expenses			Net Worth or Capital Funds on This Financial Statement _____		
Net Profit from Operations			**DETAIL OF INVENTORY**		
Other Income					
Less Other Expense			Is Inventory Figure Actual or Estimated? _____		
Net Profit Before Income Tax			By Whom Taken or Estimated _____ When? _____		
Federal and State Income Tax			Buy Principally From _____		
Net Profit or Loss			Average Terms of Purchase _____ Sale _____		
(To Net Worth or Earned Surplus)			Time of Year Inventory Maximum _____ Minimum _____		

SCHEDULE A   LIST OF REAL ESTATE AND IMPROVEMENTS WITH ENCUMBRANCES THEREON

DESCRIPTION, STREET NUMBER, LOCATION	TITLE IN NAMES OF	BOOK VALUE		MORTGAGES OR LIENS		TERMS OF PAYMENT	HOLDER OF LIEN
		LAND	IMPROVEMENTS	MATURITY	AMOUNT		
		$	$		$	$	
TOTALS		$	$		$	$	

SCHEDULE B   STOCKS & BONDS: Describe Fully. Use Supplemental Sheet if Necessary. Indicate if Stocks Are Common or Preferred. Give Interest Rate and Maturity of Bonds.

NO. OF SHARES AMT. OF BONDS	NAME AND ISSUE (DESCRIBE FULLY)	BOOK VALUE		MARKET VALUE	
		LISTED	UNLISTED	PRICE	VALUE
		$	$		$
	TOTALS	$	$		$

SCHEDULE C   Complete if Statement is for an Individual or Sole Proprietorship

Age _____ Number of Years in Present Business _____ Date of Filing Fictitious Trade Style _____

What Property Listed in This Statement is in Joint Tenancy? _____ Name of Other Party _____

What Property Listed in This Statement is Community Property? _____ Name of Other Party _____

With What Other Business Are You Connected? _____ Have You Filed Homestead? _____

Do You Deal With or Carry Accounts With Stockbrokers? _____ Amount $ _____ Name of Firm _____

SCHEDULE D   Complete if Statement is of a Partnership

NAME OF PARTNERS (INDICATE SPECIAL PARTNERS)	AGE	AMOUNT CONTRIBUTED	OUTSIDE NET WORTH	OTHER BUSINESS CONNECTIONS
		$	$	

Date of Organization _____ Limited or General? _____ Terminates _____

If Operating Under Fictitious Trade Style, Give Date of Filing _____

SCHEDULE E   Complete if Statement is of a Corporation

	AUTHORIZED	PAR VALUE	OUTSTANDING		ISSUED FOR	
			SHARES	AMOUNT	CASH	OTHER (DESCRIBE)
Common Stock	$	$		$	$	
Preferred Stock	$	$		$	$	

Bonds—Total Issue $ _____ Outstanding $ _____ Due _____ Interest Rate _____

Date Incorporated _____ Under Laws of State of _____

OFFICERS	AGE	SHARES OWNED		DIRECTORS AND PRINCIPAL STOCKHOLDERS	SHARES OWNED	
		COMMON	PREFERRED		COMMON	PREFERRED
President				Director		
Vice President				Director		
Secretary				Director		
Treasurer						

SCHEDULE F   Complete in ALL Cases   INSURANCE

Are Your Books Audited by Outside Accountants? _____ Name _____

Date of Last Audit _____ To What Date Has the U.S. Internal Revenue Department Examined Your Books? _____

Are You Borrowing From Any Other Branch of This Bank? _____ Which? _____

Are You Applying for Credit At Any Other Source? _____ Where? _____

Have You Ever Failed in Business? _____ If So, Attach a Complete Explanation and State Basis of Settlement With Creditors _____

Lease Has _____ Years to Run, With Monthly Rental of $ _____

Merchandise _____ $ _____
Machinery & Fixtures _____ $ _____
Buildings _____ $ _____
Earthquake _____ $ _____
Is Extended Coverage Endorsement Included? _____
Do You Carry Workmen's Compensation Insurance? _____

Automobiles and Trucks:
Public Liability $ _____ M/$ _____ M
Collision _____ $ _____
Property Damage _____ $ _____
Life Insurance _____ $ _____
Name of Beneficiary _____

STATEMENT OF BANK OFFICER:
Insofar as our records reveal, this Financial Statement is accurate and true. The foregoing statement is (a copy of) the original signed by the maker, in the credit files of this Bank.

_____ ASSISTANT CASHIER-MANAGER

The undersigned solemnly declares and certifies that the above statement (or in lieu thereof, the attached statement, as the case may be) and supporting schedules, both printed and written, give a full, true, and correct statement of the financial condition of the undersigned as of the date indicated.

Signature _____

By _____

(TITLE, IF CORPORATION)

SAMPLE FINANCIAL STATEMENT
(Personal)

PERSONAL FINANCIAL STATEMENT
(DO NOT USE FOR BUSINESS)

As of _____ _____ 19 _____

Received at _____ Branch

Name _____

Employed by _____ Years _____

Address _____

Position _____ Age _____ Name of Spouse _____

If Employed Less Than
1 Year, Previous Employer _____

The undersigned, for the purpose of procuring and establishing credit from time to time with you and to induce you to permit the undersigned to become indebted to you on notes, endorsements, guarantees, overdrafts or otherwise, furnishes the following (or in lieu thereof the attached) which is the most recent statement prepared by or for the undersigned as being a full, true and correct statement of the financial condition of the undersigned on the date indicated, and agrees to notify you immediately of the extent and character of any material change in said financial condition, and also agrees that if the undersigned, or any endorser or guarantor of any of the obligations of the undersigned, at any time fails in business or becomes insolvent, or commits an act of bankruptcy, or dies, or if a writ of attachment, garnishment, execution or other legal process be issued against property of the undersigned or if any assessment for taxes against the undersigned, other than taxes on real property, is made by the federal or state government or any department thereof, or if any of the representations made below prove to be untrue, or if the undersigned fails to notify you of any material change as above agreed, or if such change occurs, or if the business, or any interest therein, of the undersigned is sold, then and in such case, all of the obligations of the undersigned to you or held by you shall immediately be due and payable, without demand or notice. This statement shall be construed by you to be a continuing statement of the condition of the undersigned, and a new and original statement of all assets and liabilities upon each and every transaction in and by which the undersigned hereafter becomes indebted to you, until the undersigned advises in writing to the contrary.

ASSETS	DOLLARS	cents	LIABILITIES	DOLLARS	cents
Cash in B of _____ (Branch)			Notes payable B of _____ (Branch)		
Cash in _____ (Other - give name)			Notes payable _____ (Other)		
Accounts Receivable-Good _____			Accounts payable _____		
Stocks and Bonds (Schedule B) _____			Taxes payable _____		
Notes Receivable-Good _____			Contracts payable _____ (To whom)		
Cash Surrender Value Life Insurance _____			Contracts payable _____ (To whom)		
Autos _____ (Year-Make) (Year-Make)			Real Estate indebtedness (Schedule A) _____		
Real Estate (Schedule A) _____			Other Liabilities (describe)		
Other Assets (describe)			1. _____		
1. _____			2. _____		
2. _____			3. _____		
3. _____			4. _____		
4. _____			TOTAL LIABILITIES NET WORTH		
5. _____					
TOTAL ASSETS			TOTAL		

ANNUAL INCOME			and ANNUAL EXPENDITURES (Excluding Ordinary living expenses)		
Salary _____			Real Estate payment (s) _____		
Salary (wife or husband) _____			Rent _____		
Securities Income _____			Income Taxes _____		
Rentals _____			Insurance Premiums _____		
Other (describe)			Property Taxes _____		
1. _____			Other (describe-include instalment payments other than real estate)		
2. _____			1. _____		
3. _____			2. _____		
4. _____			3. _____		
5. _____					
TOTAL INCOME			TOTAL EXPENDITURES		

LESS-TOTAL EXPENDITURES

NET CASH INCOME
(exclusive of ordinary living expenses) _____

What assets in this statement are in joint tenancy? _____ Name of other Party _____

Have you filed homestead? _____

Are you a guarantor on anyone's debt? _____ If so, give details _____

Are any encumbered assets or debts secured except as indicated? _____ If so, please itemize by debt and security _____

Do you have any other business connections? _____ If so, give details _____

Are there any suits or judgments against you? _____ Any pending? _____

Have you gone through bankruptcy or compromised a debt? _____

Have you made a will? _____ Number of dependents _____

SCHEDULE A–REAL ESTATE

Location and type of Improvement	Title in Name of	Estimated Value	Amount Owing	To Whom Payable
			$	

SCHEDULE B–STOCKS AND BONDS

Number of Shares Amount of Bonds	Description	Current Market on Listed	Estimated Value on Unlisted
		$	$

If additional space is needed for Schedule A and/or Schedule B, list on separate sheet and attach.

INSURANCE

Life Insurance $ _____ Name of Company _____ Beneficiary _____

Automobile Insurance:
Public Liability — yes ☐ no ☐   Property Damage — yes ☐ no ☐
Comprehensive personal Liability - yes ☐ no ☐

STATEMENT OF BANK OFFICER:
Insofar as our records reveal, this Financial Statement is accurate and true. The foregoing statement is (a copy of) the original signed by the maker, in the credit files of this bank.

_____ Assistant Cashier Manager

The undersigned certifies that the above statement (or in lieu thereof, the attached statement, as the case may be) and supporting schedules, both printed and written, give a full, true, and correct statement of the financial condition of the undersigned as of the date indicated.

_____   _____
Date signed   Signature

PRO FORMA CASH FLOW STATEMENT (SAME AS BUDGET)

Cash Flow Statements are the documents that project your cash inflow and outflow over a period of time. They are commonly know as "budgets" and are used for internal planning. The Cash Flow Statement identifies when cash is expected to be received and when it must be spent to pay bills and expenses. It shows how much cash will be needed and when it will be needed. It also allows the manager to identify where the necessary cash will come from -- will it come from sales and services rendered or must it be borrowed? The Cash Flow Projection deals only with actual cash transactions and not with depreciation and amortization of good will or other non-cash expense items.

HOW TO DEVELOP A PRO FORMA CASH FLOW STATEMENT

Since these statements deal with cash inflow and cash outflow, we have included two worksheets that can be utilized to develop your cash flow statement.

a. Sources of Cash Worksheet - contains all the financing sources for your business.
b. Cash to be Paid Out - lists all direct and indirect expenses to be paid out by your business.

The two worksheets must have all projections made for the same period (monthly, quarterly, or annually). The Cash Flow statement can be prepared for any period of time. It is recommended that you match the fiscal year of your business. It should be prepared on a monthly basis for the next year and revised not less that quarterly to reflect actual performance in the preceding three months of operation.

The format of a Pro Forma Cash Statement is as follows and should contain these categories:

Beginning Cash Balance	Interest Expense
Cash Receipts	Loan Repayment
Total Cash Available	Owner Draws
Cash Payments (Indirect Expenses)	Total Cash Paid Out
Direct Expenses	Cash Deficiency
Federal Income Tax	Loans Received
Other Taxes	Ending Cash Balance

The statement is divided vertically into thirteen columns, one for each month and a total column.

INFORMATION SOURCE FOR PRO FORMA CASH FLOW STATE-MENTS

If you have been in business for some time, the Sources of Cash Worksheet and the Cash to be Paid Out Worksheet can be put together from the actual figures of income and expenses of previous years combined with projected changes for the next period. If you are starting a new business, you will have to project your financial needs and predict your disbursements. This project can be made more manageable through market research at the library and by first developing several smaller individual budgets. The worksheets are then utilized to prepare the Pro Forma Cash Flow Statement. It is important that you do this job carefully as your profit at the end of the year will be dependent on the proper balance between cash inflow and outflow.

The next four pages are samples of (1) Sources of Cash Worksheet; (2) Cash to be Paid Out Worksheet; (3) Directions for completing your Pro Forma Cash Flow Statement ; and; (4) Pro Forma Cash Flow Statement.

SOURCES OF CASH WORKSHEET

(CASH FLOWING INTO YOUR BUSINESS)

1. **CASH ON HAND** $_____

2. **SALES·REVENUES**
   Sales   _____
   Service Income   _____
   Deposits on Sales or Services   _____
   Collections on Accounts Receivable   _____

3. **MISCELLANEOUS INCOME**
   Interest Income   _____

4. **SALE OF LONG-TERM ASSETS**   _____

5. **LIABILITIES**
   Loans (Banks, Finance Cos., S.B.A., etc.)   _____

6. **EQUITY**
   Owner Investments (Sole Prop. or Partnership)   _____
   Contributed Capital (Corporation)   _____
   Sale of Stock (Corporation)   _____
   Venture Capital   _____

          TOTAL CASH AVAILABLE. . . . . $_____

CASH TO BE PAID OUT WORKSHEET
(CASH FLOWING OUT OF YOUR BUSINESS)

START-UP COSTS:
    Business License (annual expense $ _____
    DBA Filing Fee (one-time cost)   _____
    Other start-up costs:

    _____   _____
    _____   _____
    _____   _____

INVENTORY PURCHASES   _____
    Cash out for items for resale or services

SELLING EXPENSE (DIRECT EXPENSE)
    Advertising   _____
    Freight   _____
    Packaging Costs   _____
    Parts & Supplies   _____
    Sales Salaries   _____
    Misc. Direct Exp.   _____
  TOTAL DIRECT EXPENSE   _____

OPERATING EXPENSE (INDIRECT EXPENSE)
    Depreciation Expense   _____
    Insurance   _____
    Licenses & Permits   _____
    Office Salaries   _____
    Rent Expense   _____
    Utilities   _____
    Miscell. Indirect Exp. _____
  TOTAL INDIRECT EXPENSE   _____

ASSETS (LONG-TERM PURCHASES)   _____
    Cash to be paid in current period

LIABILITIES   _____
    Cash outlay for retiring debts, loans,
    and/or accounts payable

OWNER EQUITY   _____
    Cash to be withdrawn by owner

      TOTAL CASH TO BE PAID OUT . . . . . $ _____

Note: Be sure to use the same time period throughout your worksheets---
      monthly, quarterly annually.

DIRECTIONS FOR COMPLETING YOUR

PRO FORMA CASH FLOW STATEMENT

Note:
1. <u>Horizontal columns</u> are divided into the twelve months and preceded by a "Total Column."

2. <u>Vertical positions of the statement</u> contain all the sources of cash and cash to be paid out. These figures are retrieved from the two previous worksheets and from Individual Budgets.

The figures are projected for each month reflecting the flow of cash in and out of your business for a one-year period. Begin with January and proceed as follows:

1. Project the Beginning Cash Balance. Enter that figure under the heading "January".

2. Project Cash Receipts for January.

3. Add the Beginning Cash Balance and the Cash Receipts to determine the Cash Available.

4. Project the Expenses, Taxes, Loan Repayments and Draws to be made in January.

5. Total the Expenses to determine Total Cash Paid Out.

6. Subtract Cash Paid Out from Total Cash Available.

7. If the result of No. 6 is a negative, enter under Cash Deficiency.

8. Anticipate any Loans to be Received and enter.

9. Add anticipated loans to cash remaining after expenses (or Cash Deficiency) to project the Ending Cash Balance for January.

10. The Ending Cash Balance for January is carried to February and becomes the February Beginning Cash Balance.

11. The process is repeated until December is completed.

To Complete "TOTAL COLUMN":

1. The Beginning Cash Balance for January is entered in the first space of the "Total Column."

2. The monthly figures for each category are added horizontally and the result entered in the corresponding category under Total.

3. The Total Column is computed in the same manner as the individual months. If you have been accurate in your computation the December Ending Cash Balance will be exactly the same as the Total Ending Cash Balance.

This process may seem complicated, but as you work with it, I think it will begin to make perfect sense and will be a straight-forward and reasonable task to accomplish.

PRO FORMA CASH FLOW STATEMENT

FOR THE YEAR 19___	TOTAL	JAN	FEB	MAR	APR	MAY	JUN	JUL	AUG	SEP	OCT	NOV	DEC
BEG. CASH BALANCE....													
CASH RECEIPTS........													
TOTAL CASH AVAILABLE													
CASH PAYMENTS													
Purchases..........													
Operating Expense...													
DIRECT EXPENSES													
Labor..............													
Materials..........													
Freight............													
Packaging..........													
Sales Expense......													
Miscell Expense.....													
FEDERAL INCOME TAX.													
OTHER TAXES........													
INTEREST EXPENSE...													
LOAN REPAYMENT.....													
OWNER'S DRAWS......													
TOTAL CASH PAID OUT													
CASH DEFICIENCY.....													
BANK LOANS RECEIVED													
ENDING CASH BALANCE													

QUARTERLY BUDGET ANALYSIS

The Quarterly Budget Analysis is a form to be used as a record for comparing your Budget with your Business's actual performance. Its purpose is to let you know whether or not you are operating within your projections and to help you maintain control of all phases of your business operations. This analysis is used to help you revise your budget on a quarterly basis to reflect actual performance in the preceding quarter. For example, if you have underbudgeted in a particular area for the first quarter and think it is indicative of the future, you will have to compensate by cutting the budget in another area.

HOW TO DEVELOP A QUARTERLY BUDGET ANALYSIS

The Quarterly Budget Analysis needs six columns. They are as follows:

Budget Item   Year-to-Date Budget
Amount Budgeted Year-to-Date Spent
Variation this Quarter Variation Year-to-Date

INFORMATION SOURCE FOR QUARTERLY BUDGET ANALYSIS

All items contained in the Budget are listed in this form. The second column is the amount budgeted for the current quarter. By subtracting the amount actually spent, you will arrive at the Variation for the Quarter. The last three columns are for year-to-date figures. If your analysis is for the 3rd Quarter, those three columns will contain figures representing the first nine months of the fiscal year.

Note: See page 67 for a Sample Quarterly Budget Analysis.

Note: The PRO FORMA CASH FLOW STATEMENT discussed and illustrated previously will also serve as your BUDGET for the new fiscal year. The form on this page is a record to be used as a means of comparing your Budget with your business's actual performance. Its purpose is to let you know whether or not you are operating withing your projections and to help you maintain control of all phases of your business operations.

For the Quarter Ending _____, 19___.

YTD = year-to-date

Budget Item	Amount Budgeted	Variation This Quarter	YTD Budget	Spent YTD	Variation YTD

THREE-YEAR PROJECTION

The Three-Year Projection is a pro forma statement projecting the future income and expenses of your business. There is some difference of opinion as to the period of time that should be covered. We suggest a three-year period. If you are applying for a loan, your potential lender may require a different time period.

HOW TO DEVELOP A THREE-YEAR PROJECTION

This pro forma statement follows very much the same format as a Profit and Loss or Income Statement. It must contain:

> **INCOME** - Net Sales, Cost of Sales, Gross Profit Services Income, and Miscellaneous Income

> **EXPENSES** - Direct and Indirect

> **NET PROFIT (LOSS) BEFORE TAXES**

> **TAXES**

> **NET PROFIT (LOSS) AFTER TAXES**

INFORMATION SOURCES OF THREE-YEAR PROJECTION

If you have been in business for a period of time, use your past financial statements to help you determine what you project for the future of your business. If you are a new business, you will have to carefully work out your figures after you have considered your business and marketing analysis. Be sure to take into account fluctuations anticipated in costs, efficiency of operation and changes in your marketing. Increases in income and expenses are only realistic and should be accounted for . Don't forget to consider that not only should your volume of sales increase, but your expenses will increase as well. These rises should be reflected in your projection. It is probably reasonable to assume that your estimates should show an approximate 10% increase per year in most areas. Do not forget to take into consideration, too, the areas in specific industries that see a decline in projections. The computer industry is a prime example of a product that has seen a marked decrease in sale price due to standardization of the micro chip and extreme competition.

For your own use, your projection statement can be compiled on a month by month basis and then compared with actual monthly performance. The SBA's Form 1009 (4-82) is very useful in this regard. Prepared in this manner, it will compile into an annual projection for your next fiscal year.

A sample of a Three-Year Projection Form can be seen on page 69.

THREE - YEAR PROJECTION

	YEAR 1	YEAR 2	YEAR 3
INCOME			
1. NET SALES (Gross - Ret. & Allow.)			
2. Cost of Goods Sold			
a. Inventory (January 1st)			
b. Purchases			
c. Cost of goods avail. for sale (a.+b.)			
d. Deduct Inventory December 31st			
3. GROSS PROFIT ON SALES			
EXPENSES			
1. Selling Expense (Direct or Controllable)			
a. Advertising			
b. Freight			
c. Legal Fees			
d. Packaging Costs			
e. Parts & Supplies			
f. Sales Salaries			
g. Miscellaneous Direct Expenses			
2. Administrative Expense (Indirect, Fixed)			
a. Depreciation Expense			
b. Insurance			
c. Loan Repayments (+Interest)			
d. Office Salaries			
e. Rent Expense			
f. Taxes & Licenses			
g. Utilities			
h. Miscellaneous Indirect Expenses			
TOTAL EXPENSES			
INCOME FROM OPERATIONS (Inc. less Exp.)			
OTHER INCOME			
1. Interest Income			
OTHER EXPENSE			
1. Interest Expense			
NET PROFIT (LOSS) BEFORE INCOME TAXES			
INCOME TAXES			
NET PROFIT (LOSS) AFTER INCOME TAXES			

Note: All figures in this projection should show approx. 10% increase per year. Also be aware that some figures may decrease due to trends in your particular industry.

BREAK-EVEN ANALYSIS

The Break-Even Analysis predicts the point at which a company's expenses will exactly match the sales or service volume. It is the point at which the business will neither make a profit nor incur a loss. The Break-Even Point can be calculated either in mathematical or graph form. It can be expressed in: (a) Total dollars of revenue exactly offset by total expenses or; (b) Total units of production (the cost of which exactly equals the income divided by their sale).

HOW TO DEVELOP A BREAK-EVEN ANALYSIS

To apply a break-even analysis to an operation, two types of expenses must first be figured: (1) **Fixed operating expense for the period (Indirect expense)**; (2) **Variable operating expense for that same period (Cost of Goods sold + Direct expense)**. These costs are further explained on the form. Fixed costs do not vary with sales or output, but remain at the same constant level. Variable expenses increase or decrease in direct portion to the output. The greater the volume of sales, the higher the cost. To complete your break-even analysis, it will be necessary to determine your anticipated Total Revenues · Sales. This figure should realistically be in terms of a reasonable spread.

INFORMATION SOURCE FOR BREAK-EVEN ANALYSIS

Estimates of the three figures needed to compute this analysis may be taken directly from the Three-Year Projection.

MATHEMATICALLY, a firm's sales at Break-Even Point can be computed by using the following formula:

$$\text{Break-Even Point Sales} = \text{Fixed Operation Expense} + \left[\frac{\text{Cost of Goods Sold}}{\text{Total Sales} \cdot \text{Revenues}} \times \text{Sales} \right]$$

Let us assume: a. Fixed Expenses = $25,000
            b. Variable Expenses Sold = $45,000
            c. Total Sales Volume = $90,000

Using the above formula, the actual figures would be:

$$\text{Break-Even Point Sales} = \$25,000 + \left[\frac{\$45,000}{\$90,000} \, S \right]$$

Break-Even Point (S) = $25,000 + 1/2 S
S - 1/2 S = $25,000
1/2 S = $25,000
S = $50,000 (Break-Even Point: neither profit nor loss)

GRAPHICALLY, a firm's sales at Break-Even Point can be plotted as described on the next page.

Recordkeeping: The Secret to Growth and Profit

BREAK-EVEN POINT GRAPH

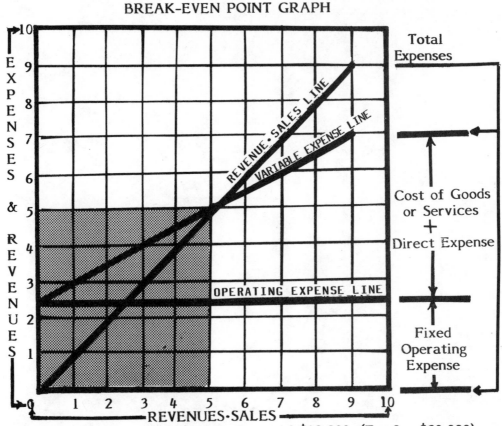

Note: The figures shown are expressed in terms of $10,000. (Ex: 2 = $20,000)

To Complete the Graph, you must find the following:

1. **Fixed Operating Expense for Period** – Those expenses not related directly to the production of your product (fixed or indirect costs). Includes rent, insurance, office expenses, depreciation, etc. **$25,000 in this example**

2. **Variable Expense** – Costs associated with the production and selling of your goods or services (cost of goods sold + direct expenses). Include inventory purchases, labor, materials, freight, packaging costs, sales commissions, etc. These costs may be expressed by multiplying the unit cost by the units to be sold. **EX: 30,000 units @ $3.00 = $90,000**

3. **Total Revenues·Sales** – This is the figure representing the units to be sold multiplied by sale price per unit. **Ex: 30,000 units @ $3.00 = $90,000**

To Draw Graph Lines:

1. **Draw Horizontal Line** representing Fixed Operating Expense (2.5).

2. **Draw Variable Expense Line** from left end of Fixed Operating Expense Line, sloping upward to the point where Total Expenses on the vertical scale (7) meet total revenues.sales on the horizontal scale (9).

3. **Draw Revenues·Sales Line** from zero through point describing the total Revenues·Sales on both scales (9). Note: Same point on both scales (9).

Break-Even Point – The point on the graph where the Variable Expense Line intersects the Revenue·Sales Line. This business will break even at the time sales volume reaches $50,000. The triangular area below that point represents company losses. The triangular area above the point represents potential profit.

5

TAXES AND RECORDKEEPING

5. TAXES AND RECORDKEEPING

WARNING -- DISCLAIMER

This chapter is intended to provide information in regard to the subject matter covered. It is presented with the understanding that we are in no way rendering legal, accounting or other professional services. Our purpose is to introduce you to some of the common tax forms and publications and to provide you with a general guide for use in recordkeeping. Detailed information, along with legal advice, will have to be obtained from your accountant, attorney, or the IRS.

BASIC UNDERSTANDING OF THE U.S. TAX SYSTEM

If you are going to be in command of your business recordkeeping, it will be necessary for you to have a good basic understanding of the relationship between your finances and income tax accounting. When the Federal income tax came into being, it was structured according to accounting principles. This has served a double purpose. The records you keep enable you to retrieve the necessary information for filing taxes at the close of your tax year. By the same token, the tax forms that you will be required to submit will provide you with important clues as to how your records can be set up, not only in a usable format, but in a manner that will make it practical for you to analyze your records and determine what changes will have to be implemented for future growth and profit.

COMPREHENDING THE RELATIONSHIP BETWEEN TAX FORMS AND BUSINESS ANALYSIS

In order for you to better comprehend the relationship between the Tax System and analyzing your business, we will give you two examples of tax forms and how you can benefit from understanding those forms.

SCHEDULE C. (FORM 1040)

Entitled *Profit or (Loss) from Business or Profession* (required tax reporting form for Sole Proprietors).

IRS INFORMATION REQUIRED

Gross receipts or sales, beginning and ending inventories, labor, materials, goods purchased, returns and allowances, deductions, and net profit or loss.

BENEFITS OF UNDERSTANDING

In order to provide the year-end information required on a Schedule C, it will be necessary for you to set up a recordkeeping system that includes a General Journal, Petty Cash Record, and Inventory Records. An examination of the Deduction Categories will help you to determine the indirect expense categories to be used in your General Journal. It will also tell you how to sort out Petty Cash expenses for final retrieval. In order to derive the figures for Gross Income, you will have to set up categories for keeping the direct expenses in the General Journal--and categories for types of income as well. Year end totals of these expenses are used to develop Profit and Loss Statements and Balance Sheets--the two most important of the Financial Statements used to analyze your business.

> **Note:** Form 1065 - *U.S. Partnership Return of Income* and Form 1120 or Form 1120-A, *U.S. Corporation Income Tax Returns*, are used for those legal structures.

SCHEDULE SE (FORM 1040)

Entitled *Computation of Social Security Self-Employment Tax*

IRS INFORMATION REQUIRED

Computation of business contribution to social security.

BENEFITS OF UNDERSTANDING

Failure to familiarize yourself with the requirements on how to compute this tax and know what percentage of your net income will be owed will result in a false picture as to the net profit of your business. Don't forget-- the IRS is interested in your Net Profit **before** taxes. You are concerned with Net Profit **after** taxes.

As you can see from the above examples, examination of required tax forms can lead to the discovery of many types of records that you will need and profit from in your business.

FEDERAL TAXES FOR WHICH YOU MAY BE LIABLE

The next section of this chapter will be devoted to introducing you to the most common federal taxes for which a sole proprietor, partnership, or corporation may be liable.

We will discuss each briefly as to:

- a. Tax to be reported.
- b. Forms used for reporting.
- c. IRS Publications to be used for information.

Each discussion will be followed by samples of the reporting forms to be filed.

INCOME TAX (FOR SOLE PROPRIETORS)

File Schedule C (Form 1040), *Profit or (Loss) from Business or Profession*.

If you are a sole proprietor, you report your income and expenses from your business or profession on Schedule C. File Schedule C with your Form 1040 and report the amount of net profit or (loss) from Schedule C on your 1040. If you operate more than one business as a sole proprietor, you prepare a separate Schedule C for each business.

You are a sole proprietor if you are self-employed and are the sole owner of an unincorporated business.

SCHEDULE C AND FORM 1040

These forms are due by April 15th. If you use a fiscal year, your return is due by the 15th day of the 4th month after the close of your tax year.

IRS PUBLICATION

See Publication 334, *Tax Guide for Small Business* (Rev. Nov. 87). Chapter 27 discusses tax rules and Chapter 38 will illustrate how to fill in this form.

SCHEDULE C

This is one of the most helpful tax forms to be used in setting up your records. If you will examine the information needed, you will be able to use this form to derive categories for your General Journal. It will also illustrate the need for maintaining inventories and depreciation schedules.

SAMPLE

Schedule C (Form 1040) can be seen on the next two pages.

SCHEDULE C
(Form 1040)

Department of the Treasury
Internal Revenue Service (3)

Profit or (Loss) From Business or Profession
(Sole Proprietorship)

Partnerships, Joint Ventures, etc., Must File Form 1065.

▶ Attach to Form 1040, Form 1041, or Form 1041S. ▶ See Instructions for Schedule C (Form 1040).

OMB No. 1545-0074

19**87**

Attachment
Sequence No. **09**

Name of proprietor

Social security number (SSN)

A Principal business or profession, including product or service (see Instructions)

B Principal business code
(from Part IV) ▶

C Business name and address ▶ ....

D Employer ID number (Not SSN)

E Method(s) used to value closing inventory:
   (1) ☐ Cost   **(2)** ☐ Lower of cost or market   **(3)** ☐ Other (attach explanation)

		Yes	No
F	Accounting method: **(1)** ☐ Cash **(2)** ☐ Accrual **(3)** ☐ Other (specify) ▶		
G	Was there any change in determining quantities, costs, or valuations between opening and closing inventory? (If "Yes," attach explanation.)		
H	Are you deducting expenses for an office in your home?		
I	Did you file **Form 941** for this business for any quarter in 1987?		
J	Did you "materially participate" in the operation of this business during 1987? (If "No," see Instructions for limitations on losses.)		
K	Was this business in operation at the end of 1987?		
L	How many months was this business in operation during 1987? ▶		

M If this schedule includes a loss, credit, deduction, income, or other tax benefit relating to a tax shelter required to be registered, check here. ▶ ☐
   If you check this box, you **MUST** attach **Form 8271.**

Part I Income

1a Gross receipts or sales	1a	
b Less: Returns and allowances	1b	
c Subtract line 1b from line 1a and enter the balance here	1c	
2 Cost of goods sold and/or operations (from Part III, line 8)	2	
3 Subtract line 2 from line 1c and enter the **gross profit** here	3	
4 Other income (including windfall profit tax credit or refund received in 1987)	4	
5 Add lines 3 and 4. This is the **gross income** ▶	5	

Part II Deductions

6 Advertising		23 Repairs		
7 Bad debts from sales or services (see Instructions.)		24 Supplies (not included in Part III)		
		25 Taxes		
8 Bank service charges		26 Travel, meals, and entertainment:		
9 Car and truck expenses		a Travel		
10 Commissions		b Total meals and entertainment		
11 Depletion		c Enter 20% of line 26b subject to limitations (see Instructions)		
12 Depreciation and section 179 deduction from Form 4562 (not included in Part III)				
13 Dues and publications		d Subtract line 26c from 26b		
14 Employee benefit programs		27 Utilities and telephone		
15 Freight (not included in Part III)		28a Wages		
16 Insurance		b Jobs credit		
17 Interest:		c Subtract line 28b from 28a		
a Mortgage (paid to financial institutions)		29 Other expenses (list type and amount):		
b Other		....		
18 Laundry and cleaning		....		
19 Legal and professional services		....		
20 Office expense		....		
21 Pension and profit-sharing plans		....		
22 Rent on business property				

30 Add amounts in columns for lines 6 through 29. These are the **total deductions** ▶	30	

31 **Net profit or (loss).** Subtract line 30 from line 5. If a profit, enter here and on Form 1040, line 13, and on Schedule SE, line 2 (or line 5 of Form 1041 or Form 1041S). If a loss, you **MUST** go on to line 32 ... | **31** |

32 If you have a loss, you **MUST** answer this question: "Do you have amounts for which you are not at risk in this business?" (See Instructions.) ☐ Yes ☐ No
   If "Yes," you **MUST** attach **Form 6198.** If "No," enter the loss on Form 1040, line 13, and on Schedule SE, line 2 (or line 5 of Form 1041 or Form 1041S).

For Paperwork Reduction Act Notice, see Form 1040 Instructions.

Schedule C (Form 1040) 1987

Schedule C (Form 1040) 1987   Page **2**

Part III   Cost of Goods Sold and/or Operations (See Schedule C Instructions for Part III)

1	Inventory at beginning of year. (If different from last year's closing inventory, attach explanation.)	1
2	Purchases less cost of items withdrawn for personal use	2
3	Cost of labor. (Do not include salary paid to yourself.)	3
4	Materials and supplies	4
5	Other costs	5
6	Add lines 1 through 5	6
7	Less: Inventory at end of year	7
8	Cost of goods sold and/or operations. Subtract line 7 from line 6. Enter here and in Part I, line 2	8

Part IV   Codes for Principal Business or Professional Activity

Locate the major business category that best describes your activity (for example, Retail Trade, Services, etc.). Within the major category, select the activity code that identifies (or most closely identifies) the business or profession that is the principal source of your sales or receipts. **Enter this 4-digit code on line B on page 1 of Schedule C. (Note:** *If your principal source of income is from farming activities, you should file* **Schedule F (Form 1040), Farm Income and** *Expenses.)*

Construction

Code

0018   Operative builders (building for own account)

General contractors

0034   Residential building
0059   Nonresidential building
0075   Highway and street construction
3889   Other heavy construction (pipe laying, bridge construction, etc.)

Building trade contractors, including repairs

0232   Plumbing, heating, air conditioning
0257   Painting and paper hanging
0273   Electrical work
0299   Masonry, dry wall, stone, tile
0414   Carpentering and flooring
0430   Roofing, siding, and sheet metal
0455   Concrete work
0471   Water well drilling
0885   Other building trade contractors (excavation, glazing, etc.)

Manufacturing, Including Printing and Publishing

0612   Bakeries selling at retail
0638   Other food products and beverages
0653   Textile mill products
0679   Apparel and other textile products
0695   Leather, footware, handbags, etc.
0810   Furniture and fixtures
0836   Lumber and other wood products
0851   Printing and publishing
0877   Paper and allied products
0893   Chemicals and allied products
1016   Rubber and plastics products
1032   Stone, clay, and glass products
1057   Primary metal industries
1073   Fabricated metal products
1099   Machinery and machine shops
1115   Electric and electronic equipment
1313   Transportation equipment
1339   Instruments and related products
1883   Other manufacturing industries

Mining and Mineral Extraction

1511   Metal mining
1537   Coal mining
1552   Oil and gas
1719   Quarrying and nonmetallic mining

Agricultural Services, Forestry, and Fishing

1917   Soil preparation services
1933   Crop services
1958   Veterinary services, including pets
1974   Livestock breeding
1990   Other animal services
2113   Farm labor and management services
2212   Horticulture and landscaping
2238   Forestry, except logging
0836   Logging
2279   Fishing, hunting, and trapping

Wholesale Trade—Selling Goods to Other Businesses, Government, or Institutions, etc.

Durable goods, including machinery, equipment, wood, metals, etc.

2618   Selling for your own account

Code

2634   Agent or broker for other firms— more than 50% of gross sales on commission

Nondurable goods, including food, fiber, chemicals, etc.

2659   Selling for your own account
2675   Agent or broker for other firms— more than 50% of gross sales on commission

Retail Trade—Selling Goods to Individuals and Households

3012   Selling door-to-door, by telephone or party plan, or from mobile unit
3038   Catalog or mail order
3053   Vending machine selling

Selling From Store, Showroom, or Other Fixed Location

Food, beverages, and drugs

3079   Eating places (meals or snacks)
3095   Drinking places (alcoholic beverages)
3210   Grocery stores (general line)
0612   Bakeries selling at retail
3236   Other food stores (meat, produce, candy, etc.)
3251   Liquor stores
3277   Drug stores

Automotive and service stations

3319   New car dealers (franchised)
3335   Used car dealers
3517   Other automotive dealers (motorcycles, recreational vehicles, etc.)
3533   Tires, accessories, and parts
3558   Gasoline service stations

General merchandise, apparel, and furniture

3715   Variety stores
3731   Other general merchandise stores
3756   Shoe stores
3772   Men's and boys' clothing stores
3913   Women's ready-to-wear stores
3921   Women's accessory and specialty stores and furriers
3939   Family clothing stores
3954   Other apparel and accessory stores
3970   Furniture stores
3996   TV, audio, and electronics
3988   Computer and software stores
4119   Household appliance stores
4317   Other home furnishing stores (china, floor coverings, drapes, etc.)
4333   Music and record stores

Building, hardware, and garden supply

4416   Building materials dealers
4432   Paint, glass, and wallpaper stores
4457   Hardware stores
4473   Nurseries and garden supply stores

Other retail stores

4614   Used merchandise and antique stores (except used motor vehicle parts)
4630   Gift, novelty, and souvenir shops
4655   Florists
4671   Jewelry stores

Code

4697   Sporting goods and bicycle shops
4812   Boat dealers
4838   Hobby, toy, and game shops
4853   Camera and photo supply stores
4879   Optical goods stores
4895   Luggage and leather goods stores
5017   Book stores, excluding newsstands
5033   Stationery stores
5058   Fabric and needlework stores
5074   Mobile home dealers
5090   Fuel dealers (except gasoline)
5884   Other retail stores

Real Estate, Insurance, Finance, and Related Services

5512   Real estate agents and managers
5538   Operators and lessors of buildings (except developers)
5553   Operators and lessors of other real property (except developers)
5710   Subdividers and developers, except cemeteries
5736   Insurance agents and services
5751   Security and commodity brokers, dealers, and investment services
5777   Other real estate, insurance, and financial activities

Transportation, Communications, Public Utilities, and Related Services

6114   Taxicabs
6312   Bus and limousine transportation
6338   Trucking (except trash collection)
6510   Trash collection without own dump
6536   Public warehousing
6551   Water transportation
6619   Air transportation
6635   Travel agents and tour operators
6650   Other transportation and related services
6676   Communication services
6692   Utilities, including dumps, snowplowing, road cleaning, etc.

Services (Providing Personal, Professional, and Business Services)

Hotels and other lodging places

7096   Hotels, motels, and tourist homes
7211   Rooming and boarding houses
7237   Camps and camping parks

Laundry and cleaning services

7419   Coin-operated laundries and dry cleaning
7435   Other laundry, dry cleaning, and garment services
7450   Carpet and upholstery cleaning
7476   Janitorial and related services (building, house, and window cleaning)

Business and/or personal services

7617   Legal services (or lawyer)
7633   Income tax preparation
7658   Accounting and bookkeeping
7674   Engineering, surveying, and architectural

Code

7690   Management, consulting, and public relations
7716   Advertising, except direct mail
7732   Employment agencies and personnel supply
7757   Computer and data processing, including repair and leasing
7773   Equipment rental and leasing (except computer and automotive)
7914   Investigative and protective services
7880   Other business services

Personal services

8110   Beauty shops (or beautician)
8318   Barber shop (or barber)
8334   Photographic portrait studios
8516   Shoe repair and shine services
8532   Funeral services and crematories
8714   Child day care
8730   Teaching or tutoring
8755   Counseling (except health practitioners)
8771   Ministers and chaplains
6882   Other personal services

Automotive services

8813   Automotive rental or leasing, without driver
8839   Parking, except valet
8854   General automotive repairs
8870   Specialized automotive repairs (brake, body repairs, paint, etc.)
8896   Other automotive services (wash, towing, etc.)

Miscellaneous repair, except computers

9019   TV and audio equipment repair
9035   Other electrical equipment repair
9050   Reupholstery and furniture repair
2881   Other equipment repair

Medical and health services

9217   Offices and clinics of medical doctors (MD's)
9233   Offices and clinics of dentists
9258   Osteopathic physicians and surgeons
9274   Chiropractors
9290   Optometrists
9415   Registered and practical nurses
9431   Other licensed health practitioners
9456   Dental laboratories
9472   Nursing and personal care facilities
9886   Other health services

Amusement and recreational services

8557   Physical fitness facilities
9613   Videotape rental stores
9639   Motion picture theaters
9654   Other motion picture and TV film and tape activities
9670   Bowling alleys
9696   Professional sports and racing, including promoters and managers
9811   Theatrical performers, musicians, agents, producers, and related services
9837   Other amusement and recreational services

8888   Unable to classify

INCOME TAX (FOR PARTNERSHIPS)

File Form 1065, *U.S. Partnership Return of Income.*

Every partnership doing business in or having income from sources within the United States is required to file Form 1065 for its tax year. This is mainly an information return.

A partnership is the relationship between two or more persons who join together to carry on a trade or business with each person contributing money, property, labor, or skill, and each expecting to share in the profits and losses of the business.

Partnership profits are not taxed to the partnership. Each partner must take into account, separately, his distributive share of partnership items and report it on his own income tax return.

SCHEDULES K AND K-1 (FORM 1065)

These forms are used to show partners' distributive shares of reportable partnership items. Form 1065 and its Schedules K or K-1 are filed separately and not attached to your income tax return.

SCHEDULE E (FORM 1040), SUPPLEMENTAL INCOME SCHEDULE, PART II

This is used to report partnership items on your individual tax return. Failure to treat your individual and partnership returns consistently will allow the IRS to assess and take action to collect deficiencies and penalties.

IRS PUBLICATIONS

See Publication 334, *Tax Guide for Small Business* (Rev. Nov., 87), Chapters 3, 28, and 29.

SAMPLE

Form 1065 and Schedule K follows on pages 81 and 82.

Form **1065** Department of the Treasury Internal Revenue Service	**U.S. Partnership Return of Income** ▶ **For Paperwork Reduction Act Notice, see Form 1065 Instructions.** For calendar year 1987, or fiscal year beginning _____ , 1987, and ending _____ , 19 ___	OMB No. 1545-0099 **1987**

A Principal business activity	Use IRS label. Other- wise, please print or type.	Name	D Employer identification number
B Principal product or service		Number and street (or P.O. Box number if mail is not delivered to street address)	E Date business started
C Business code number		City or town, state, and ZIP code	F Enter total assets at end of tax year $

G Check accounting method: (1) ☐ Cash (2) ☐ Accrual (3) ☐ Other

H Check applicable boxes: (1) ☐ Final return (2) ☐ Change in address (3) ☐ Amended return

		Yes	No
I Number of partners in this partnership ▶ _____			
J Is this partnership a limited partnership (see the Instructions)? . .			
K Is this partnership a partner in another partnership?			
L Are any partners in this partnership also partnerships?			
M Does the partnership meet **all** the requirements shown in the Instructions for Question M?			
N Was there a distribution of property or a transfer (for example, by sale or death) of a partnership interest during the tax year? If "Yes," see the Instructions concerning an election to adjust the basis of the partnership's assets under section 754			

	Yes	No
O At any time during the tax year, did the partnership have an interest in or a signature or other authority over a financial account in a foreign country (such as a bank account, securities account, or other financial account)? (See the Instructions for exceptions and filing requirements for Form TD F 90-22.1.) If "Yes," write the name of the foreign country. ▶ _____		
P Was the partnership the grantor of, or transferor to, a foreign trust which existed during the current tax year, whether or not the partnership or any partner has any beneficial interest in it? If "Yes," you may have to file Forms 3520, 3520-A, or 926 . .		
Q Was this partnership in operation at the end of 1987?		
R Number of months in 1987 that this partnership was in operation ▶ _____		
S Check this box if the partnership has filed or is required to file Form 8264, Application for Registration of a Tax Shelter . . . . ☐		
T Check this box if this is a partnership subject to the consolidated partnership audit procedures of TEFRA. (See page 7 of the Instructions.) . . . . . ☐		

Caution: *Include **only** trade or business income and expenses on lines 1a–21 below. See the instructions for more information.*

Income

1a	Gross receipts or sales $ _____ 1b Minus returns and allowances $ _____ Balance ▶	1c	
2	Cost of goods sold and/or operations (Schedule A, line 7)	2	
3	Gross profit (subtract line 2 from line 1c)	3	
4	Ordinary income (loss) from other partnerships and fiduciaries (attach schedule) .	4	
5	Net farm profit (loss) (attach Schedule F (Form 1040))	5	
6	Net gain (loss) (Form 4797, line 18)	6	
7	Other income (loss)	7	
8	**TOTAL** income (loss) (combine lines 3 through 7)	8	

Deductions *(see instructions for limitations)*

9a	Salaries and wages (other than to partners) $ _____ 9b Minus jobs credit $ _____ Balance ▶	9c	
10	Guaranteed payments to partners	10	
11	Rent	11	
12	Deductible interest expense not claimed elsewhere on return (see Instructions) . .	12	
13	Taxes	13	
14	Bad debts	14	
15	Repairs	15	
16a	Depreciation from Form 4562 (attach Form 4562) $ _____ 16b Minus depreciation claimed on Schedule A and elsewhere on return $ _____ Balance ▶	16c	
17	Depletion (**Do not deduct oil and gas depletion.**)	17	
18a	Retirement plans, etc.	18a	
b	Employee benefit programs	18b	
19	Other deductions (attach schedule)	19	
20	**TOTAL** deductions (add amounts in column for lines 9c through 19)	20	
21	Ordinary income (loss) from trade or business activity(ies) (subtract line 20 from line 8) . . .	21	

Please Sign Here

Under penalties of perjury, I declare that I have examined this return, including accompanying schedules and statements, and to the best of my knowledge and belief, it is true, correct, and complete. Declaration of preparer (other than taxpayer) is based on all information of which preparer has any knowledge.

▶ _____ ▶ _____
Signature of general partner   Date

Paid Preparer's Use Only

Preparer's signature ▶		Date	Check if self-employed ▶ ☐	Preparer's social security no.
Firm's name (or yours if self-employed) and address ▶			E.I. No. ▶	
			ZIP code ▶	

FORM 1065 - SCHEDULE K

PARTNERS' DISTRIBUTIVE SHARES OF INCOME - SAMPLE

Form 1065 (1987)   Page **3**

Schedule K	Partners' Shares of Income, Credits, Deductions, etc.		
	(a) Distributive share items		**(b) Total amount**

Income (Loss)	**1** Ordinary income (loss) from trade or business activity(ies) (page 1, line 21)	**1**	
	2 Net income (loss) from rental real estate activity(ies) (Schedule H, line 17)	**2**	
	3a Gross income from other rental activity(ies)	**3a** $	
	b Minus expenses (attach schedule)	**3b** $	
	c Balance net income (loss) from other rental activity(ies) . . . . ▶	**3c**	
	4 Portfolio income (loss):		
	a Interest income	**4a**	
	b Dividend income	**4b**	
	c Royalty income	**4c**	
	d Net short-term capital gain (loss) (Schedule D, line 4)	**4d**	
	e Net long-term capital gain (loss) (Schedule D, line 9)	**4e**	
	f Other portfolio income (loss) (attach schedule)	**4f**	
	5 Guaranteed payments	**5**	
	6 Net gain (loss) under section 1231 (other than due to casualty or theft)	**6**	
	7 Other (attach schedule)	**7**	
Deductions	**8** Charitable contributions (attach list)	**8**	
	9 Expense deduction for recovery property (section 179)	**9**	
	10 Deductions related to portfolio income (do not include investment interest expense) . . .	**10**	
	11 Other (attach schedule)	**11**	
Credits	**12a** Credit for income tax withheld	**12a**	
	b Low-income housing credit (attach Form 8586)	**12b**	
	c Qualified rehabilitation expenditures related to rental real estate activity(ies) (attach schedule)	**12c**	
	d Credit(s) related to rental real estate activity(ies) other than 12b and 12c (attach schedule)	**12d**	
	e Credit(s) related to rental activity(ies) other than 12b, 12c, and 12d (attach schedule) . . .	**12e**	
	13 Other (attach schedule)	**13**	
Self-Employment	**14a** Net earnings (loss) from self-employment	**14a**	
	b Gross farming or fishing income	**14b**	
	c Gross nonfarm income	**14c**	
Tax Preference Items	**15a** Accelerated depreciation of real property placed in service before 1/1/87	**15a**	
	b Accelerated depreciation of leased personal property placed in service before 1/1/87 . .	**15b**	
	c Depreciation adjustment on property placed in service after 12/31/86	**15c**	
	d Depletion (other than oil and gas)	**15d**	
	e (1) Gross income from oil, gas, and geothermal properties	**15e(1)**	
	(2) Deductions allocable to oil, gas, and geothermal properties	**15e(2)**	
	f Other (attach schedule)	**15f**	
Investment Interest	**16a** Interest expense on investment debts	**16a**	
	b (1) Investment income included on lines 4a through 4f, Schedule K	**16b(1)**	
	(2) Investment expenses included on line 10, Schedule K	**16b(2)**	
Foreign Taxes	**17a** Type of income _____		
	b Foreign country or U.S. possession _____		
	c Total gross income from sources outside the U.S. (attach schedule)	**17c**	
	d Total applicable deductions and losses (attach schedule)	**17d**	
	e Total foreign taxes (check one): ▶ ☐ Paid ☐ Accrued	**17e**	
	f Reduction in taxes available for credit (attach schedule)	**17f**	
	g Other (attach schedule)	**17g**	
Other	**18** Attach schedule for other items and amounts not reported above. See Instructions . . .		

INCOME TAX (S CORPORATIONS)

File Form 1120S, *U.S. Income Tax Return* for an S Corporation.

Some corporations may elect not to be subject to income tax. If a corporation qualifies and chooses to become an S corporation, its income usually will be taxed to the shareholders.

The formation of an S corporation is only allowable under certain circumstances. It can be an advantageous form of legal structure, but if entered into without careful planning, it can result in more taxes instead of less, as anticipated.

Form 1120S is used to file an income tax return for an S corporation. Schedule K and K-1 are extremely important parts of Form 1120S. Schedule K summarizes the corporation's income, deductions, credits, etc., reportable by the shareholders. Schedule K-1 shows each shareholder's separate share. The individual shareholder reports his income tax on Form 1040.

Form 1120S is due on the 15th day of the third month after the end of the tax year.

IRS PUBLICATIONS
The following publications available for use are:

    a. Publication 589, *Tax Information on S Corporations*
    b. Publication 334 (Rev. Nov., 87), *Tax Guide for Small Business*

SAMPLE
A copy of form 1120S follows.

Form 1120S

Department of the Treasury
Internal Revenue Service

U.S. Income Tax Return for an S Corporation

For the calendar year 1987 or tax year beginning _____ , 1987, ending _____ , 19 ____

▶ For Paperwork Reduction Act Notice, see page 1 of the Instructions.

OMB No. 1545-0130

1987

A Date of election as an S corporation

B Business code no. (see Specific Instructions)

Use IRS label. Otherwise, please print or type.

Name

Number and street (P.O. Box number if mail is not delivered to street address)

City or town, state, and ZIP code

C Employer identification number

D Date incorporated

E Total assets (see Specific Instructions)
Dollars | Cents
$

F Check applicable boxes: (1) ☐ Initial return (2) ☐ Final return (3) ☐ Change in address (4) ☐ Amended return

G Check this box if this is an S corporation subject to the consolidated audit procedures of sections 6241 through 6245 (see instructions) . . . . ▶ ☐

H Was this corporation in operation at the end of 1987 (see instructions)? . . . . Yes ☐ No ☐

I How many months in 1987 was this corporation in operation (see instructions)? . . . . ▶

Caution: Include **only** trade or business income and expenses on lines 1a through 21. See the instructions for more information.

Income

1a Gross receipts or sales _____ **b** Less returns and allowances _____ Balance ▶	**1c**	
2 Cost of goods sold and/or operations (Schedule A, line 7).	**2**	
3 Gross profit (subtract line 2 from line 1c)	**3**	
4 Net gain (or loss) from Form 4797, line 18 (see instructions)	**4**	
5 Other income (see instructions—attach schedule)	**5**	
6 TOTAL income (loss)—Combine lines 3, 4 and 5 and enter here . . . . . . ▶	**6**	

Deductions (See instructions for limitations.)

7 Compensation of officers	**7**	
8a Salaries and wages _____ **b** Less jobs credit _____ Balance ▶	**8c**	
9 Repairs.	**9**	
10 Bad debts (see instructions)	**10**	
11 Rents	**11**	
12 Taxes	**12**	
13 Deductible interest expense not claimed or reported elsewhere on return (see instructions) . .	**13**	
14a Depreciation from Form 4562 (attach Form 4562). **14a**		
b Depreciation reported on Schedule A and elsewhere on return . . **14b**		
c Subtract line 14b from line 14a	**14c**	
15 Depletion (**Do not deduct oil and gas depletion. See instructions.**)	**15**	
16 Advertising	**16**	
17 Pension, profit-sharing, etc. plans	**17**	
18 Employee benefit programs	**18**	
19 Other deductions (attach schedule)	**19**	
20 TOTAL deductions—Add lines 7 through 19 and enter here . . . . ▶	**20**	
21 Ordinary income (loss) from trade or business activity(ies)—Subtract line 20 from line 6 . . .	**21**	

Tax and Payments

22 Tax:		
a Excess net passive income tax (attach schedule) **22a**		
b Tax from Schedule D (Form 1120S) **22b**		
c Add lines 22a and 22b	**22c**	
23 Payments:		
a Tax deposited with Form 7004 . . . . **23a**		
b Credit for Federal tax on gasoline and special fuels (attach Form 4136) . **23b**		
c Add lines 23a and 23b	**23c**	
24 TAX DUE (subtract line 23c from line 22c). See instructions for Paying the Tax . . . . ▶	**24**	
25 OVERPAYMENT (subtract line 22c from line 23c). . . . . ▶	**25**	

Please Sign Here

Under penalties of perjury, I declare that I have examined this return, including accompanying schedules and statements, and to the best of my knowledge and belief, it is true, correct, and complete. Declaration of preparer (other than taxpayer) is based on all information of which preparer has any knowledge.

▶ _____
Signature of officer | Date | ▶ _____ Title

Paid Preparer's Use Only

Preparer's signature ▶	Date	Check if self-employed ▶ ☐	Preparer's social security number
Firm's name (or yours if self-employed) and address ▶		E.I. No. ▶	
		ZIP code ▶	

Form **1120S** (1987)

INCOME TAX (CORPORATIONS)

File Form 1120 or 1120-A, *Corporation Income Tax Return*, or *Corporations Short-Form Income Tax Return.*

Every corporation, unless it is specifically exempt or has dissolved, must file a tax return even if it has no taxable income for the year and regardless of the amount of its gross income for the year.

Form 1120 or 1120-A is used to report corporation income tax. It is due on March 15th. A corporation using a fiscal year not beginning January 1st and ending December 31st, will have to file it on or before the 15th of the third month following the close of its fiscal year.

IRS PUBLICATIONS

See publication 334 (Rev. Nov., 1987), Chapter 29 for explanation of the application of various tax provisions to corporations (filing requirements, tax computations, estimated tax payments, corporate distribution, and retained earnings. For a more complete discussion of corporation taxation, as well as liquidations and stock redemptions, see Publication 541 *Tax Information on Corporations.*

SAMPLE

See Forms 1120 and 1120A on the following pages.

Form **1120**	**U.S. Corporation Income Tax Return**	OMB No. 1545-0123
Department of the Treasury Internal Revenue Service	For calendar 1987 or tax year beginning _____, 1987, ending _____, 19 ____ ▶ For Paperwork Reduction Act Notice, see page 1 of the instructions.	19**87**

Check if a—	Use IRS label. Otherwise please print or type.	Name	D Employer Identification number
A Consolidated return ☐			
B Personal Holding Co. ☐		Number and street	E Date incorporated
C Business Code No. (See the list in the instructions.)		City or town, state, and ZIP code	F Total assets (See Specific Instructions.)

F Total assets: Dollars | Cents

G Check applicable boxes: (1) ☐ Initial return (2) ☐ Final return (3) ☐ Change in address

$ _____

Income

1a	Gross receipts or sales _____ b Less returns and allowances _____ Balance ▶	1c
2	Cost of goods sold and/or operations (Schedule A)	2
3	Gross profit (line 1c less line 2)	3
4	Dividends (Schedule C)	4
5	Interest	5
6	Gross rents	6
7	Gross royalties	7
8	Capital gain net income (attach separate Schedule D)	8
9	Net gain or (loss) from Form 4797, line 18, Part II (attach Form 4797)	9
10	Other income (see instructions—attach schedule)	10
11	TOTAL income—Add lines 3 through 10 and enter here . . . . ▶	11

Deductions (See Instructions for limitations on deductions)

12	Compensation of officers (Schedule E)	12
13a	Salaries and wages _____ b Less jobs credit _____ Balance ▶	13c
14	Repairs	14
15	Bad debts (see instructions)	15
16	Rents	16
17	Taxes	17
18	Interest	18
19	Contributions (see Instructions for 10% limitation)	19
20	Depreciation (attach Form 4562) 20	
21	Less depreciation claimed in Schedule A and elsewhere on return . 21a	21b
22	Depletion	22
23	Advertising	23
24	Pension, profit-sharing, etc., plans	24
25	Employee benefit programs	25
26	Other deductions (attach schedule)	26
27	TOTAL deductions—Add lines 12 through 26 and enter here · · · ▶	27
28	Taxable income before net operating loss deduction and special deductions (line 11 less line 27) ·	28
29	Less: a Net operating loss deduction (see instructions) 29a	
	b Special deductions (Schedule C) 29b	29c

Tax and Payments

30	Taxable income (line 28 less line 29c)	30
31	TOTAL TAX (Schedule J)	31
32	Payments: a 1986 overpayment credited to 1987	
b	1987 estimated tax payments	
c	Less 1987 refund applied for on Form 4466 . ( )	
d	Tax deposited with Form 7004	
e	Credit from regulated investment companies (attach Form 2439) .	
f	Credit for Federal tax on gasoline and special fuels (attach Form 4136) .	32
33	Enter any PENALTY for underpayment of estimated tax—check ▶ ☐ if Form 2220 is attached	33
34	TAX DUE—If the total of lines 31 and 33 is larger than line 32, enter AMOUNT OWED	34
35	OVERPAYMENT—If line 32 is larger than the total of lines 31 and 33, enter AMOUNT OVERPAID	35
36	Enter amount of line 35 you want: Credited to 1988 estimated tax ▶ _____ Refunded ▶	36

Please Sign Here

Under penalties of perjury, I declare that I have examined this return, including accompanying schedules and statements, and to the best of my knowledge and belief, it is true, correct, and complete. Declaration of preparer (other than taxpayer) is based on all information of which preparer has any knowledge.

▶ _____ Signature of officer | Date | ▶ _____ Title

Paid Preparer's Use Only

Preparer's signature ▶	Date	Check if self-employed ☐	Preparer's social security number
Firm's name (or yours, if self-employed) and address ▶		E.I. No. ▶	
		ZIP code ▶	

SAMPLE FORM 1120-A

U.S. CORPORATION SHORT-FORM INCOME TAX RETURN

Form 1120-A

Department of the Treasury
Internal Revenue Service

U.S. Corporation Short-Form Income Tax Return
To see if you qualify to file Form 1120-A, see instructions.

For calendar 1987 or tax year beginning _____, 1987, ending _____, 19 ___

1235

OMB No. 1545-0890

1987

See Instructions for list of principal business:

A Activity

B Product or service

C Code

Use IRS label. Otherwise, please type or machine print

Name

Number and street

City or town, state, and ZIP code

D Employer identification number (EIN)

E Date incorporated

F Total assets (See Specific Instructions.)

	Dollars	Cents
$		

G Check method of accounting: **(1)** ☐ Cash **(2)** ☐ Accrual **(3)** ☐ Other (specify) . . ▶

H Check applicable boxes: **(1)** ☐ Initial return **(2)** ☐ Change in address

Income

1a	Gross receipts or sales	**b** Less returns and allowances _____ Balance ▶	**1c**
2	Cost of goods sold and/or operations (see instructions)		**2**
3	Gross profit (line 1c less line 2)		**3**
4	Domestic corporation dividends subject to the Section 243(a)(1) deduction		**4**
5	Interest		**5**
6	Gross rents		**6**
7	Gross royalties		**7**
8	Capital gain net income (attach separate Schedule D (Form 1120))		**8**
9	Net gain or (loss) from Form 4797, line 18, Part II (attach Form 4797)		**9**
10	Other income (see instructions)		**10**
11	TOTAL income—Add lines 3 through 10		**11**

Deductions (See instructions for limitations on deductions)

12	Compensation of officers (see instructions)		**12**
13a	Salaries and wages _____ **b** Less jobs credit _____ Balance ▶		**13c**
14	Repairs		**14**
15	Bad debts (see instructions)		**15**
16	Rents		**16**
17	Taxes		**17**
18	Interest		**18**
19	Contributions (see instructions for 10% limitation)		**19**
20	Depreciation (attach Form 4562)	**20**	
21	Less depreciation claimed elsewhere on return	**21a**	**21b**
22	Other deductions (attach schedule)		**22**
23	TOTAL deductions—Add lines 12 through 22		**23**
24	Taxable income before net operating loss deduction and special deductions (line 11 less line 23)		**24**
25	**Less: a** Net operating loss deduction (see instructions)	**25a**	
	b Special deductions (see instructions)	**25b**	**25c**

26	Taxable income (line 24 less line 25c)	**26**
27	TOTAL TAX (from Part I, line 6 on page 2)	**27**

Tax and Payments

28	**Payments:**	
a	1986 overpayment allowed as a credit	
b	1987 estimated tax payments	
c	Less 1987 refund applied for on Form 4466 . . ( )	
d	Tax deposited with Form 7004	
e	Credit from regulated investment companies (attach Form 2439)	
f	Credit for Federal tax on gasoline and special fuels (attach Form 4136) . . .	**28**
29	Enter any **PENALTY** for underpayment of estimated tax—Check ▶ ☐ if Form 2220 is attached . .	**29**
30	**TAX DUE**—If the total of lines 27 and 29 is larger than line 28, enter AMOUNT OWED	**30**
31	**OVERPAYMENT**—If line 28 is larger than the total of lines 27 and 29, enter AMOUNT OVERPAID	**31**
32	Enter amount of line 31 you want: **Credited to 1988 estimated tax** ▶ _____ Refunded ▶	**32**

Please Sign Here

Under penalties of perjury, I declare that I have examined this return, including accompanying schedules and statements, and to the best of my knowledge and belief, it is true, correct, and complete. Declaration of preparer (other than taxpayer) is based on all information of which preparer has any knowledge.

▶ _____ Signature of officer _____ Date _____ Title

Paid Preparer's Use Only

Preparer's signature	Date	Check if self-employed ▶ ☐	Preparer's social security number
Firm's name (or yours if self-employed) and address		E.I. No. ▶ ZIP code ▶	

For Paperwork Reduction Act Notice, see page 1 of the Instructions.

Form **1120-A** (1987)

Taxes and Recordkeeping

87

ESTIMATED TAX (FOR SOLE PROPRIETORS AND INDIVIDUALS WHO ARE PARTNERS OR S CORPORATION SHAREHOLDERS)

File Form 1040-ES, *Estimated Tax for Individuals*.

If you are a sole proprietor, an individual who is a partner, or a shareholder in an S Corporation, you probably will have to make estimated tax payments if the total of your estimated income tax and self-employment tax is in excess of a certain amount (in 1988, if it exceeds your total withholding and credits by $500 or more).

Underpayment of estimated taxes may result in a penalty on the amount not paid.

Form 1040-ES is used to estimate your tax. It is filed on the 15th day of the 4th, 6th, and 9th months of the tax year, and 15th day of the 1st month after the end of the tax year. Use an Estimated Tax Worksheet to figure estimated taxes. Keep it for your own records and revise if your actual income is very far over or under your estimate. After the first filing, Form 1040-ES will be sent to you each year.

PUBLICATIONS
See Publication 505, *Tax Withholding and Estimated Tax*, for information. Also see the instructions accompanying Form 1040-ES.

SAMPLE
See samples of an Estimated Tax Worksheet and a 1040-ES can be seen on the following pages .

SAMPLE

1988 ESTIMATED TAX WORKSHEET

	1988 Estimated Tax Worksheet (Keep for Your Records—Do Not Send to Internal Revenue Service)			
1	Enter amount of Adjusted Gross Income you expect in 1988	1		
2	If you plan to itemize deductions, enter the estimated total of your deductions. If you do not plan to itemize deductions, see **Standard Deduction** on page 3. Enter the amount here	2		
3	Subtract line 2 from line 1. Enter the difference here	3		
4	Exemptions (multiply $1,950 times number of personal exemptions). If you are eligible to be claimed as a dependent on another person's return, see **Personal Exemption** on page 3	4		
5	Subtract line 4 from line 3	5		
6	Tax. (Figure your tax on line 5 by using Tax Rate Schedule X, Y, or Z in these instructions. DO NOT use the Tax Table or Tax Rate Schedule X, Y, or Z in the 1987 Form 1040 Instructions.)	6		
7	Enter any additional taxes (see line 7 Instructions)	7		
8	Add lines 6 and 7.	8		
9	Credits (see line 9 Instructions)	9		
10	Subtract line 9 from line 8	10		
11	Self-employment tax. Estimate of 1988 self-employment income $_____; if $45,000 or more, enter $5,859; **if less, multiply the amount by .1302** (see line 11 Instructions)	11		
12	Other taxes (see line 12 Instructions)	12		
13a	Total. Add lines 10 through 12	13a		
b	Earned income credit and credit from **Form 4136**	13b		
c	Total. Subtract line 13b from line 13a	13c		
14a	Enter 90% (66⅔% for farmers and fishermen) of line 13c	14a		
b	Enter 100% of the tax shown on your 1987 tax return	14b		
c	Enter the smaller of lines 14a or 14b. This is your required annual payment	14c		
	Caution: *Generally, if you do not prepay at least the amount on line 14c, you may be subject to a penalty for not paying enough estimated tax. To avoid a penalty, make sure your estimate on line 13c is as accurate as possible. If you are unsure of your estimate and line 14a is smaller than line 14b, you may want to pay up to the amount shown on line 14b. For more information, get Publication 505.*			
15	Income tax withheld and estimated to be withheld (including income tax withholding on pensions, annuities, certain deferred income, etc.) during 1988	15		
16	Balance (subtract line 15 from line 14c). (**Note:** If line 13c less line 15 is less than $500, you are not required to make estimated tax payments.) If you are applying an overpayment from 1987 to 1988 estimated tax, see Instruction C(2), page 1 .	16		
17	If the first payment you are required to make is due April 15, 1988, enter ¼ of line 16 (less any 1987 overpayment that you are applying to this installment) here and on line 1 of your payment-voucher(s). You may round off cents to the nearest whole dollar	17		
	Amended Estimated Tax Schedule (Use if your estimated tax changes during the year)			
1	Amended estimated tax	1		
2a	Amount of 1987 overpayment chosen for credit to 1988 estimated tax and applied to date	2a		
b	Estimated tax payments to date	2b		
c	Total of lines 2a and 2b	2c		
3	Unpaid balance (subtract line 2c from line 1).	3		
4	Amount to be paid (see Instructions D (1) and E)	4		

Page 5

FORM 1040-ES

ESTIMATED TAXES – SAMPLE VOUCHERS

Form **1040-ES**

Department of the Treasury
Internal Revenue Service

1988
Payment-
Voucher

Return this voucher with check or money order payable to the Internal Revenue Service. Please write your social security number and "1988 Form 1040-ES" on your check or money order. Please do not send cash. Enclose, but do not staple or attach, your payment with this voucher.
File only if you are making a payment of estimated tax.

OMB No. 1545-0087
Expires 9-30-90

(Calendar year—Due Sept. 15, 1988)

	Your first name and initial	Your last name	Your social security number
1 Amount of payment $ _____	(If joint payment, complete for spouse) Spouse's first name and initial	Spouse's last name if different from yours	If joint payment, spouse's social security number
2 Fiscal year filers enter year ending _____ (month and year)	Address (number and street)		
	City, state, and ZIP code		

Please type or print

For Paperwork Reduction Act Notice, see instructions on page 1.

Tear off here

Form **1040-ES**

Department of the Treasury
Internal Revenue Service

1988
Payment-
Voucher

Return this voucher with check or money order payable to the Internal Revenue Service. Please write your social security number and "1988 Form 1040-ES" on your check or money order. Please do not send cash. Enclose, but do not staple or attach, your payment with this voucher.
File only if you are making a payment of estimated tax.

OMB No. 1545-0087
Expires 9-30-90

(Calendar year—Due June 15, 1988)

	Your first name and initial	Your last name	Your social security number
1 Amount of payment $ _____	(If joint payment, complete for spouse) Spouse's first name and initial	Spouse's last name if different from yours	If joint payment, spouse's social security number
2 Fiscal year filers enter year ending _____ (month and year)	Address (number and street)		
	City, state, and ZIP code		

Please type or print

For Paperwork Reduction Act Notice, see instructions on page 1.

Tear off here

Form **1040-ES**

Department of the Treasury
Internal Revenue Service

1988
Payment-
Voucher

Return this voucher with check or money order payable to the Internal Revenue Service. Please write your social security number and "1988 Form 1040-ES" on your check or money order. Please do not send cash. Enclose, but do not staple or attach, your payment with this voucher.
File only if you are making a payment of estimated tax.

OMB No. 1545-0087
Expires 9-30-90

(Calendar year—Due April 15, 1988)

	Your first name and initial	Your last name	Your social security number
1 Amount of payment $ _____	(If joint payment, complete for spouse) Spouse's first name and initial	Spouse's last name if different from yours	If joint payment, spouse's social security number
2 Fiscal year filers enter year ending _____ (month and year)	Address (number and street)		
	City, state, and ZIP code		

Please type or print

For Paperwork Reduction Act Notice, see instructions on page 1.   Page 7

☆ U.S. GOVERNMENT PRINTING OFFICE: 1987-0-183-141 E.I. NO: 94-2249262

ESTIMATED TAX (FOR CORPORATIONS)

File Form 1120-W, *Corporation Estimated Tax (Worksheet)*.

A corporation's estimated tax is the amount of its expected tax liability (including alternative minimum tax and environmental tax) less its allowable tax credits. At the time of this writing, every corporation whose estimated tax is expected to be $40 or more is required to make estimated tax payments.

DEPOSITS

If a corporation's estimated tax is $40 or more, its estimated tax payments must be deposited with an authorized financial institution or a Federal Reserve Bank. Each deposit must be accompanied by a federal tax deposit coupon and deposited according to the instructions in the coupon book.

The due dates of deposits are the 15th day of the 4th, 6th, 9th and 12th months of the tax year. Depending on when the $40 requirement is first met, a corporation will make either 4, 3, 2, or 1 installment deposits. Amounts of estimated tax should be refigured each quarter and amended to reflect changes.

FORM 1120-W (WORKSHEET)

This form is filled out as an aid in determining the estimated tax and required deposits. The form should be retained and not filed with IRS. As an aid in determining its estimated alternative minimum tax and environmental tax, a corporation should get a copy of Form 4626-W. Retain this form and do not file with IRS.

IRS PUBLICATION

See Publication 334, *Tax Guide for Small Business* (Rev. Nov., 87), Chapter 29. For a more complete discussion of corporation taxation, as well as liquidations and stock redemptions, see Publication 542, T*ax Information on Corporations*.

SAMPLE

See Sample of Form 1120-W (Worksheet) on the following page.

FORM 1120-W

CORPORATION ESTIMATED TAX – SAMPLE WORKSHEET

Form **1120-W** (WORKSHEET) Department of the Treasury Internal Revenue Service	**Corporation Estimated Tax** (Do not file—keep for your records.)	OMB No. 1545-0975 **1988**

1	Taxable income expected in the tax year	1	
2	Enter the smaller of line 1 or $50,000 (members of a controlled group, see instructions)	2	
3	Subtract line 2 from line 1	3	
4	Enter the smaller of line 3 or $25,000 (members of a controlled group, see instructions)	4	
5	Subtract line 4 from line 3	5	
6	15% of line 2	6	
7	25% of line 4	7	
8	34% of line 5	8	
9	If line 1 is greater than $100,000, enter the lesser of: 5% of the excess over $100,000; or $11,750 (members of a controlled group, see instructions)	9	
10	Add amounts on lines 6 through 9	10	
11	Estimated tax credits	11	
12	Subtract line 11 from line 10	12	
13	Tax from refiguring a prior year investment credit	13	
14a	Alternative minimum tax	14a	
b	Environmental tax	14b	
15	Total—Add lines 12 through 14b	15	
16	Credit for Federal tax on gasoline and special fuels.	16	
17	Estimated tax—Subtract line 16 from line 15	17	
18	Divide line 17 by the number of installments to be paid for the tax year. This is the amount due for each installment. A corporation may elect to apply its 1987 overpayment against its 1988 tax. Generally, the overpayment will be applied against the earliest installment unless the taxpayer instructs the IRS differently. See Rev. Rul. 84-58, 1984-1 C.B. 254	18	

Amended Estimated Tax

If, after the corporation figures and deposits estimated tax, it finds that its estimated tax is much more or less than originally estimated because its economic condition has changed, it should refigure its estimated tax before the next installment. Corporations may use the following lines to figure the remaining installment payments. (See instructions for exceptions.)

19	Refigured estimated tax for 1988		19	
20	Amount of 1987 overpayment elected as a credit against 1988 estimated tax	20	
21	Earlier estimated tax payments made for 1988 (include only net amounts deposited—do not include the credit taken in line 20)	21	
22	Total amount already paid (add lines 20 and 21)	22	
23	Unpaid balance—Subtract line 22 from line 19	23	
24	Divide the amount on line 23 by the number of remaining installments. This is the amount due for each remaining installment	24	

For Paperwork Reduction Act Notice, see Instructions.   Form **1120-W** (1988)

SELF-EMPLOYMENT TAX (FOR SOLE PROPRIE-TOR, INDIVIDUAL WHO IS A PARTNER OR S COR-PORATION SHAREHOLDER)

File Schedule SE (Form 1040), *Computation of Social Security Self-Employment Tax.*

The self-employment tax is a social security tax for individuals who work for them-selves. Social Security benefits are available to the self-employed individual just as they are to wage earners. Your payments of self-employment tax contribute to your coverage under the social security system. That coverage provides you with retirement benefits and with medical insurance benefits.

> **Note:** You may be liable for self-employment tax even if you are now fully insured under social security and are now receiving benefits.

WHO MUST PAY THE TAX?

If you carry on a trade or business, except as an employee, you will probably have to pay self-employment tax. A trade or business is generally an activity that is carried on for a livelihood, or in good faith to make a profit. The business does not need to actually make a profit, but the profit motive **must** exist and you **must** make ongoing efforts to further your business. Regularity of activities and transactions and the production of income are key elements. You are probably self-employed if you are a (1) sole proprietor, (2) independent contractor, (3) member of a partnership, or (4) are otherwise in business for yourself.

INCOME LIMITS

At the present time (as of Jan. 1988), you must pay self-employment tax if you have net earnings from self-employment of $400 or more. The maximum amount of 1987 earnings subject to self-employment tax was $43,800. In 1988, the maximum amount of 1987 earnings subject to self-employment tax is $45,000. If you are also a wage earner and those earnings were subject to social security tax, you will not be taxed on that amount under self-employment income.

JOINT RETURNS

You may not file a joint Schedule SE (Form 1040) even if you file a joint income tax return. Your spouse is not considered self-employed just because you are. If you both have self-employment income, each of you must file a separate Schedule SE (Form 1040).

SOCIAL SECURITY NUMBER

You must have a social security number if you have to pay self-employment tax. You may apply for one at the nearest Social Security Office. The application, Form SS-5 (Application for a Social Security Number Card) may be obtained from any Social Security Office.

TAX RATES

The self-employment tax rate for 1988 is 14.3% of your net earnings from self-employment. With credits, you will pay at a net rate of 13.02%.

> **Note:** It is important here to be sure that you understand that this tax is on your net earnings **before income tax**. When you are pricing your product or service and projecting net income or (loss) after taxes, it will make a great deal of difference. On a net income before taxes of $20,000, in a 30% tax bracket, the self-employment tax on that $20,000 would be $2,640 computed on net earnings before income tax (correct) and only $11,823 computed on net earnings after income tax (incorrect). The worksheet for this computation will keep you from erring, but it is important for you to understand the concept to plan effectively.

SCHEDULE SE (FORM 1040)

Computation of Social Security Self-Employment Tax is used to compute self-employment tax. If you are required to pay estimated income tax (see Estimated Tax, section) you must also figure any self-employment tax you owe and include that amount when you send in your 1040-ES vouchers. If you are not required to pay estimated taxes, the full payment is remitted with your annual tax return.

IRS PUBLICATION

See Publication 334 (Rev. Nov., 1987), *Tax Guide for Small Business*, Chapter 33., Self-Employment Tax. Also see Publication 553, *Self-Employment Tax*, included in this publication is an illustrated Schedule SE (Form 1040).

SAMPLES

For a sample of Schedule SE (Form 1040) can be seen on the next two pages. For information on 1040-ES, refer back to pages 89 and 90.

SCHEDULE SE
(Form 1040)
Department of the Treasury
Internal Revenue Service   (3)

Computation of Social Security Self-Employment Tax

▶ See Instructions for Schedule SE (Form 1040).

▶ Attach to Form 1040.

OMB No. 1545-0074

1987

Attachment
Sequence No. 18

Name of person with **self-employment** income (as shown on social security card)

Social security number of person with **self-employment** income ▶

A If your only self-employment income was from earnings as a minister, member of a religious order, or Christian Science practitioner, AND you filed Form 4361, then DO NOT file Schedule SE. Instead, write "Exempt-Form 4361" on Form 1040, line 48. However, if you filed Form 4361, but have $400 or more of other earnings subject to self-employment tax, continue with Part I and check here ▶ ☐

B If you filed Form 4029 and have received IRS approval, DO NOT file Schedule SE. Write "Exempt-Form 4029" on Form 1040, line 48.

C If your only earnings subject to self-employment tax are wages from an electing church or church-controlled organization that is exempt from employer social security taxes and you are not a minister or a member of a religious order, skip lines 1–8. Enter zero on line 9. Continue with line 11a.

Part I   Regular Computation of Net Earnings From Self-Employment

1	Net farm profit (or loss) from Schedule F (Form 1040), line 37, and farm partnerships, Schedule K-1 (Form 1065), line 14a	**1**
2	Net profit (or loss) from Schedule C (Form 1040), line 31, and Schedule K-1 (Form 1065), line 14a (other than farming). (See Instructions for other income to report.) Employees of an electing church or church-controlled organization DO NOT enter your Form W-2 wages on line 2. See the Instructions . .	**2**

Part II   Optional Computation of Net Earnings From Self-Employment (See "Who Can Use Schedule SE" in the Instructions.)

See Instructions for limitations. Generally, this part may be used **only** if you meet any of the following tests:

A Your **gross** farm income¹ was not more than $2,400; **or**

B Your **gross** farm income¹ was more than $2,400 and your **net** farm profits² were **less** than $1,600; **or**

C Your **net** nonfarm profits³ were less than $1,600 and your **net** nonfarm profits³ were also **less** than two-thirds (⅔) of your **gross** nonfarm income.⁴

Note: If line 2 above is two-thirds (⅔) or more of your gross nonfarm income⁴, or, if line 2 is $1,600 or more, you may **not** use the optional method.
¹From Schedule F (Form 1040), line 12, and Schedule K-1 (Form 1065), line 14b.   ³From Schedule C (Form 1040), line 31, and Schedule K-1 (Form 1065), line 14a.
²From Schedule F (Form 1040), line 37, and Schedule K-1 (Form 1065), line 14a.   ⁴From Schedule C (Form 1040), line 5, and Schedule K-1 (Form 1065), line 14c.

3	Maximum income for optional methods	**3**	$1,600 00
4	Farm Optional Method—If you meet test A or B above, enter the **smaller of:** two-thirds (⅔) of gross farm income from Schedule F (Form 1040), line 12, and farm partnerships, Schedule K-1 (Form 1065), line 14b; **or** $1,600 . . .	**4**	
5	Subtract line 4 from line 3	**5**	
6	Nonfarm Optional Method—If you meet test C above, enter the **smallest of:** two-thirds (⅔) of gross nonfarm income from Schedule C (Form 1040), line 5, and Schedule K-1 (Form 1065), line 14c (other than farming); **or** $1,600; **or,** if you elected the farm optional method, the amount on line 5	**6**	

Part III   Computation of Social Security Self-Employment Tax

7	Enter the amount from Part I, line 1, **or,** if you elected the farm optional method, Part II, line 4	**7**	
8	Enter the amount from Part I, line 2, **or,** if you elected the nonfarm optional method, Part II, line 6 . . .	**8**	
9	Add lines 7 and 8. If less than $400, do not file this schedule. (Exception: If you are an employee of an electing church or church-controlled organization and the total of lines 7 and 8 is less than $400, enter zero and complete the rest of this schedule.) . . .	**9**	
10	The largest amount of combined wages and self-employment earnings subject to social security or railroad retirement tax (tier 1) for 1987 is	**10**	$43,800 00

11a Total social security wages and tips from Forms W-2 and railroad retirement compensation (tier 1). **Note:** Medicare qualified government employees whose wages are only subject to the 1.45% medicare (hospital insurance benefits) tax and employees of certain church or church-controlled organizations should **not** include those wages on this line. (See Instructions.) . . . . | **11a** |

b Unreported tips subject to social security tax from Form 4137, line 9, or to railroad retirement tax (tier 1) . . . . | **11b** |

c Add lines 11a and 11b | **11c** |

12a Subtract line 11c from line 10. (If zero or less, enter zero.) | **12a** |

b Enter your medicare qualified government wages if you are required to use the worksheet in Part III of the Instructions . . . **12b**

c Enter your Form W-2 wages of $100 or more from an electing church or church-controlled organization . . . **12c**

d Add lines 9 and 12c. | **12d** |

13 Enter the smaller of line 12a or line 12d. . . . . | **13** |

If line 13 is $43,800, enter $5,387.40 on line 14. Otherwise, multiply line 13 by .123 and enter the result on line 14 . . . . | ×.123 |

14 Self-employment tax. Enter this amount on Form 1040, line 48 . . . . | **14** |

For Paperwork Reduction Act Notice, see Form 1040 Instructions.

Schedule SE (Form 1040) 1987

SOCIAL SECURITY (FICA) TAX AND WITHHOLDING OF INCOME TAX

File Form 941 (941E, 942 or 943), *Employer's Quarterly Federal Tax Return*. Also: W-2, W-3, and W-4.

If you have one or more employees, you will probably be required to withhold federal income tax from their wages. You also may be subject to the Social Security taxes under the Federal Insurance Contribution Act (FICA).

WHO ARE EMPLOYEES?

Under common law rules, every individual who performs services that are subject to the will and control of an employer, as to both **what** must be done and **how** it must be done, is an employee. Two of the usual characteristics of an employer-employee relationship are that the employer has the right to discharge the employee and the employer supplies tools and a place to work. It does **not** matter if the employee is called an employee, or a partner, co-adventurer, agent, or independent contractor. It does **not** matter how the payments are measured, how they are made, or what they are called. Nor does it matter whether the individual is employed full time or part time.

> Note: For an in-depth discussion and example of employer-employee relationship, see Publication 539, *Employment Taxes*. If you want the IRS to determine whether a worker is an employee, file Form SS-8 with the District Director for the area in which your business is located.

SOCIAL SECURITY TAXES

The Federal Insurance Contributions Act (FICA) provides for a federal system of old age, survivors, disability, and hospital insurance. This system is financed through social security taxes, also known as FICA taxes. Social security taxes are levied on both you and your employees. You as an employer must collect and pay the employee's part of the tax. You must withhold it from wages. You are also liable for your own (employer's) share of social security taxes. For 1988, your tax rate and your employee's tax rate are scheduled to increase to 7.51%. The wage base subject to these taxes is $45,000 for 1988. Social Security taxes and withheld income tax are reported and paid together. For more detailed information, see Publication 334, Chapter 34.

WITHHOLDING OF INCOME TAX

Generally, you must withhold income from wages you pay employees if their wages for any payroll period are more than the amount of their withholding allowance for that period. The amount to be withheld is figured separately for each payroll period. You should figure withholding on gross wages before any deductions for social security tax, pension, union dues, insurance, etc. are made. Circular E contains the applicable tables and detailed instructions for using withholding methods. Also see Publication 539 for a discussion on all methods you may use to compute withholding taxes.

TAX FORMS

The following are the forms used to report social security taxes and withheld income tax.

   a. **Form 941,** *Employees Quarterly Federal Tax Return*

      Generally, social security (FICA) taxes and withheld income tax are reported together on Form 941. Forms 941E, 942, and 943 are used for other than the usual type of employee. (See Publication 334, Chapter 34). Form 943 (for Agricultural Employees) is an annual return due one month after the end of the calendar year. The other forms are quarterly returns and are due one month after the end of each calendar quarter. Due dates are April 30, July 31, October 31, and January 31. An extra 10 days are given if taxes are deposited on time and in full.

   b. **Form 8109,** *Federal Tax Deposit Coupon*

      You generally will have to make deposits of social security taxes and withheld income taxes before the return is due. Deposits are not required for taxes reported on Form 942. You must deposit both your part and your employee's part of social security taxes. See Publication 334, *Tax Guide for Small Business*, Chapter 34, for detailed information on Deposits. Use Form 8109 to make deposits.

   c. **Form W-2**

      You must furnish copies of Form W-2 to each employee from whom income tax or social security tax has been withheld. Detailed information for preparation of this form is contained in the instructions for Forms W-2 and W-2P. Furnish copies of Form W-2 to employees as soon as possible after December 31, so they may file their income tax returns early. It **must** be sent to the employee no later than January 31st. W-2's must also be transmitted annually to the Social Security Administration (see d.)

   d. **Form W-3**

      Employers must file Form W-3 annually to transmit forms W-2 and W-2P to the Social Security Administration. These forms will be processed by the Social Security Administration, which will then furnish the Internal Revenue Service with the income tax data that it needs from the forms. Form W-3 and its attachments must be filed separately from Form 941 by the last day of February, following the calendar year for which the Forms W-2 and W-2P are prepared.

e. **Form W-4**

Each new employee should give you a form W-4 (or W-4A), *Employee's Withholding Allowance Certificate*, on or before his first day of work. The certificates must include the employee's social security number. Copies of W-4 that are required to be submitted because of a large number of allowances or claims of exemption from income tax withholding are sent in with quarterly employment tax returns (Form 941 and 941E) Withholding is then figured on gross wages before deductions for social security, tax pension, insurance, etc.

LIABILITY FOR TAX WITHHELD

You are required by law to deduct and withhold income tax from the salaries and wages of your employees. You are liable for payment of that tax to the Federal government whether or not you collect it from your employees.

PUBLICATIONS

See above text for publication references for this section.

SAMPLE

You will find samples of Form 941, W-2 and W-3 and W-4 on the following pages.

EMPLOYER'S QUARTERLY FEDERAL TAX RETURN

Form 941
(Rev. January 1987)
Department of the Treasury
Internal Revenue Service

4141

Employer's Quarterly Federal Tax Return
▶ **For Paperwork Reduction Act Notice, see page 2.**
Please type or print

OMB No. 1545-0029
Expires: 8-31-88

Your name, address, employer identification number, and calendar quarter of return. (If not correct, please change.)

If address is different from prior return, check here ▶ ☐

Name (as distinguished from trade name)	Date quarter ended
Trade name, if any	Employer identification number
Address and ZIP code	

T
FF
FD
FP
I
T

IRS Use

If you are not liable for returns in the future, check here . . . ▶ ☐   Date final wages paid . . . . ▶

Complete for First Quarter Only

1a Number of employees (except household) employed in the pay period that includes March 12th ▶ | **1a**
b If you are a subsidiary corporation AND your parent corporation files a consolidated Form 1120, enter parent corporation employer identification number (EIN) . ▶ | **1b** | –

2 Total wages and tips subject to withholding, plus other compensation . . . . ▶	**2**	
3 Total income tax withheld from wages, tips, pensions, annuities, sick pay, gambling, etc. . . . ▶	**3**	
4 Adjustment of withheld income tax for preceding quarters of calendar year (see instructions) . ▶	**4**	
5 Adjusted total of income tax withheld	**5**	
6 Taxable social security wages paid . . . . . $ _____ X 14.3% (.143) . .	**6**	
7a Taxable tips reported . . . . $ _____ X 7.15% (.0715) . .	**7a**	
b Tips deemed to be wages (see instructions) . . . $ _____ X 7.15% (.0715) . .	**7b**	
c Taxable hospital insurance wages paid . . . $ _____ X 2.9% (.029) . .	**7c**	
8 Total social security taxes (add lines 6, 7a, 7b, and 7c)	**8**	
9 Adjustment of social security taxes (see instructions for required explanation) . . . . ▶	**9**	
10 Adjusted total of social security taxes (see instructions) . . . . ▶	**10**	
11 Backup withholding (see instructions)	**11**	
12 Adjustment of backup withholding tax for preceding quarters of calendar year	**12**	
13 Adjusted total of backup withholding . . . . ▶	**13**	
14 Total taxes (add lines 5, 10, and 13)	**14**	
15 Advance earned income credit (EIC) payments, if any	**15**	
16 Net taxes (subtract line 15 from line 14). **This must equal line IV below** (plus line IV of Schedule A (Form 941) if you have treated backup withholding as a separate liability).	**16**	
17 Total deposits for quarter, including overpayment applied from a prior quarter, from your records . ▶	**17**	
18 Balance due (subtract line 17 from line 16). This should be less than $500. Pay to IRS . . . ▶	**18**	

19 If line 17 is more than line 16, enter overpayment here ▶ $ _____ and check if to be:
☐ Applied to next return or ☐ Refunded.

Record of Federal Tax Liability (Complete if line 16 is $500 or more.) See the instructions under rule 4 for details before checking these boxes.
Check only if you made eighth-monthly deposits using the 95% rule ▶ ☐   Check only if you are a first time 3-banking-day depositor ▶ ☐

Tax liability (Do not show Federal tax deposits here.)

Date wages paid	First month of quarter		Second month of quarter		Third month of quarter	
1st through 3rd	A		I		Q	
4th through 7th	B		J		R	
8th through 11th	C		K		S	
12th through 15th	D		L		T	
16th through 19th	E		M		U	
20th through 22nd	F		N		V	
23rd through 25th	G		O		W	
26th through the last	H		P		X	
Total liability for month	I		II		III	

IV Total for quarter (add lines *I*, *II*, and *III*) . . . . ▶

Under penalties of perjury, I declare that I have examined this return, including accompanying schedules and statements, and to the best of my knowledge and belief, it is true, correct, and complete.

Signature ▶ _____   Title ▶ _____   Date ▶ _____

Taxes and Recordkeeping

SAMPLE Form W-2

WAGE AND TAX STATEMENT 1987

1 Control number		
	OMB No. 1545-0008	

2 Employer's name, address, and ZIP code	3 Employer's identification number	4 Employer's state I.D. number

5 Statutory employee	Deceased	Pension plan	Legal rep.	942 emp.	Subtotal	Deferred compensation	Void
☐	☐	☐	☐	☐	☐	☐	☐

6 Allocated tips	7 Advance EIC payment

8 Employee's social security number	9 Federal income tax withheld	10 Wages, tips, other compensation	11 Social security tax withheld

12 Employee's name, address, and ZIP code	13 Social security wages	14 Social security tips
	16	16a Fringe benefits incl. in Box 10
	17 State income tax	18 State wages, tips, etc.	19 Name of state
	20 Local income tax	21 Local wages, tips, etc.	22 Name of locality

Form W-2 Wage and Tax Statement 1987
Employee's and employer's copy compared ☐

Copy 1 For State, City, or Local Tax Department

---

1 Control number		
	OMB No. 1545-0008	

2 Employer's name, address, and ZIP code	3 Employer's identification number	4 Employer's state I.D. number

5 Statutory employee	Deceased	Pension plan	Legal rep.	942 emp.	Subtotal	Deferred compensation	Void
☐	☐	☐	☐	☐	☐	☐	☐

6 Allocated tips	7 Advance EIC payment

8 Employee's social security number	9 Federal income tax withheld	10 Wages, tips, other compensation	11 Social security tax withheld

12 Employee's name, address, and ZIP code	13 Social security wages	14 Social security tips
	16	16a Fringe benefits incl. in Box 10
	17 State income tax	18 State wages, tips, etc.	19 Name of state
	20 Local income tax	21 Local wages, tips, etc.	22 Name of locality

Form W-2 Wage and Tax Statement 1987
Employee's and employer's copy compared ☐

Copy 1 For State, City, or Local Tax Department

---

1 Control number		
	OMB No. 1545-0008	

2 Employer's name, address, and ZIP code	3 Employer's identification number	4 Employer's state I.D. number

5 Statutory employee	Deceased	Pension plan	Legal rep.	942 emp.	Subtotal	Deferred compensation	Void
☐	☐	☐	☐	☐	☐	☐	☐

6 Allocated tips	7 Advance EIC payment

8 Employee's social security number	9 Federal income tax withheld	10 Wages, tips, other compensation	11 Social security tax withheld

12 Employee's name, address, and ZIP code	13 Social security wages	14 Social security tips
	16	16a Fringe benefits incl. in Box 10
	17 State income tax	18 State wages, tips, etc.	19 Name of state
	20 Local income tax	21 Local wages, tips, etc.	22 Name of locality

Form W-2 Wage and Tax Statement 1987
Employee's and employer's copy compared ☐

Copy 1 For State, City, or Local Tax Department

Recordkeeping: The Secret to Growth and Profit

TRANSMITTAL OF INCOME AND TAX STATEMENTS 1987

1 Control number		OMB No. 1545-0008			
Kind of Payer ▶	2 941/941E ☐ Military ☐ 943 ☐ CT-1 ☐ 942 ☐ Medicare gov't. emp. ☐		3	4	5 Number of statements attached
6 Allocated tips	7 Advance EIC payments		8		
9 Federal income tax withheld	10 Wages, tips, and other compensation		11 Social security tax withheld		
12 Employer's state I.D. number	13 Social security wages		14 Social security tips		
15 Employer's identification number			16 Establishment number		
17 Employer's name			18 Gross annuity, pension, etc. (Form W-2P)		
YOUR COPY			20 Taxable amount (Form W-2P)		
			21 Income tax withheld by third-party payer		
19 Employer's address and ZIP code					

Form **W-3** Transmittal of Income and Tax Statements **1987**   Department of the Treasury Internal Revenue Service

Instructions

If you issue multiple Forms W-2 to show state or local tax data, do NOT report the same Federal tax data to the Social Security Administration (SSA) on more than one Copy A.

Payers filing privately printed Forms W-2 or W-2P must file Forms W-3 that are the same width as the Forms W-2 or W-2P.

Sick Pay.—Sick pay paid to an employee by a third party such as an insurance company or trust requires special treatment at year-end because IRS reconciles an entity's Forms 941 with the Forms W-2 and W-3 filed at the end of the year. See **Circular E, Employer's Tax Guide,** for information on who should prepare Forms W-2 and W-3. If the third-party payer notifies the employer about the sick-pay payments, then the following instructions apply:

A. **Third-party payers.**—Because you withheld social security tax (and perhaps Federal income tax) from persons for whom you do not file Forms W-2, you must file a separate Form W-3 with a single "dummy" Form W-2 that shows the following information:

(a) in box 9, the total income tax withheld by you (if any) from the sick pay;

(b) in box 10, the total sick pay paid by you during 1987;

(c) in box 11, the total employee social security tax withheld and paid to the IRS on your Form 941;

(d) in box 12, the words "Third-party sick pay" in place of the employee's name; and

(e) in box 13, the total of all sick pay subject to employee social security tax. On the separate Form W-3, complete only boxes 2, 9, 10, 11, 13, 15, 17, and 19. Do **not** make an entry in box 21 of this Form W-3.

B. **Employers.**—If you had employees who received sick pay in 1987 from an insurance company or other third-party payer, you must report the following on the employees' W-2s:

(a) in box 9, any income tax withheld from the sick pay by the third-party payer;

(b) in box 10, the amount of sick pay the employee must include in income;

(c) in box 11, the employee social security tax withheld by the third-party payer;

(d) in box 13, the amount of sick pay that is subject to employer social security tax; and

(e) in box 16, the amount of any sick pay not includible in income because the employee contributed to the sick pay plan.

You can include these amounts in the Form W-2 you issue the employee showing wages, or you can give the employee a separate W-2 and state that the amounts are for third-party sick pay. In either case, you must show in box 21 of Form W-3 the total amount of income tax withheld by third-party payers, even though the amounts are included in box 9.

Forms W-2 and W-2P That You Cannot Deliver.—You will need to keep for 4 years any employee (recipient) copies of Forms W-2 and W-2P that you tried to deliver but could not.

Reporting on Magnetic Media

We encourage employers and other payers with computer capabilities to use magnetic media for filing the information on Forms W-2 and W-2P. You can get filing specifications at most SSA offices. You may also get this information by writing to the Social Security Administration, P.O. Box 2317, Baltimore, MD 21203, Attn: Magnetic Media Coordinator.

Note: You must file 1987 Forms W-2 and W-2P with SSA on magnetic media instead of using Form W-3 if you file **250 or more forms** for that year.

A. **Who Must File.**—Employers and other payers must file Form W-3 to send Copy A of Forms W-2 and W-2P.

A transmitter or sender (including a service bureau, paying agent, or disbursing agent) may sign Form W-3 for the employer or payer only if the sender:

(a) Is authorized to sign by an agency agreement (either oral, written, or implied) that is valid under state law; and

(b)(i) Is authorized by the payer (by either oral, written, or implied agreement) to ask for the taxpayer identification numbers of payees who are reported on the forms; **OR**

(ii) If the return of more than one payer is included in a single magnetic media submission, the sender has an affidavit from each payer that the payer had complied with the law in attempting to secure correct TIN's; and

(c) Writes "For (name of payer)" next to the signature.

If an authorized sender signs for the payer, the payer is still responsible for filing, when due, a correct and complete Form W-3 and attachments, and is subject to any penalties that result from not complying with these requirements.

Be sure the payer's name and employer identification number on Forms W-2, W-2P, and W-3 are the same as those used on the Form 941, 942, or 943 filed by or for the payer.

If you buy or sell a business during the year, see Rev. Proc. 84-77, 1984-2 C.B. 753, for details on who should file the employment tax returns.

B. **When To File.**—File Form W-3, with attached Copy A of Forms W-2 or W-2P, by February 29, 1988.

You may request an extension of time to file by sending a letter to the IRS National Computer Center, P.O. Box 1359, Martinsburg, WV 25401-1359. Include your name and address, TIN, phone number, number of paper or magnetic media forms involved, and the reason for delay.

Employee's Withholding Allowance Certificate

1987 Form W-4A
Department of the Treasury Internal Revenue Service

What Is Form W-4A? This form is an easier way to figure your withholding than the 4-page 1987 Form W-4. If you have already given your employer a Form W-4 this year, **do not** file a new Form W-4A unless you wish to change your withholding.

Caution: Form W-4A may cause more or less tax to be withheld from your wages than you wish because it adjusts your withholding only for pay you receive after it takes effect. If not enough tax was withheld earlier in the year, you can increase your withholding by reducing the allowances claimed on line 4 of the form or by requesting that more money be withheld on line 5 of the form.

Exemption From Withholding— Important Change in Law. If you are a dependent of another person (for example,

a student who can still be claimed on your parents' return), you are not exempt if you have any nonwage income (such as interest on savings) **and** expect your total income to be more than $500.

What Do I Need To Do? Exempt employees can skip the Worksheet and go directly to line 6 of Form W-4A. All others must complete lines A through G. Many employees can stop at line G of the Worksheet.

Nonwage Income? If you have a large amount of income from other sources (such as interest or dividends), you should consider either using the 1987 Form W-4 or making estimated tax payments using Form 1040-ES. Call 1-800-424-3676 (in Hawaii and Alaska, check your local telephone

directory) for copies of the 1987 Form W-4 and **Publication 919**, "Is My Withholding Correct?"

When Should I File? File as soon as possible to avoid underwithholding problems. If you do not file by October 1, 1987, your allowances may be adjusted to "1" if single or "2" if married and your take home pay may be reduced.

Two-Earner Couples? More Than One Job? To figure the number of allowances you may claim, combine allowances and wages from all jobs on one worksheet. File a Form W-4A with each employer, but do not claim the same allowances more than once. Your withholding will usually be more accurate if you claim all allowances on the highest paying job.

W-4A Worksheet To Figure Your Withholding Allowances

A Enter "1" for **yourself** if no one else can claim you as a dependent . . . . **A** _____

B Enter "1" if:
 1. You are single and have only one job; or
 2. You are married, have only one job, and your spouse does not work; or
 3. Your wages from a second job or your spouse's wages (or the total of both) are $2,500 or less.
 . . . . **B** _____

C Enter "1" for your **spouse** if no one else claims your spouse as a dependent . . . . **C** _____

D Enter number of **dependents** other than your spouse that you will claim on your return . . . . . . **D** _____

E Enter "1" if you want to reduce your withholding because you or your spouse is at least **age 65 or blind** and you do not plan to itemize deductions . . . . **E** _____

F Enter "1" if you want to reduce your withholding because you have at least $1,500 of **child or dependent care expenses** for which you plan to claim a credit . . . . **F** _____

G Add lines A through F and enter total here . . . . ▶ **G** _____

- If you plan to **itemize or claim other deductions** and wish to reduce your withholding, turn to the Deductions Worksheet on the back.
- If you have **more than one job or a working spouse** AND your combined earnings from all jobs exceed $25,000, or $15,000 if you are married filing a joint return, turn to the Two-Earner/Two-Job Worksheet on the back if you want to avoid having too little tax withheld.
- If **neither** of the above situations applies to you, **stop here** and enter the number from line G on line 4 of Form W-4A below.

- - - - - - - - - Cut here and give the certificate to your employer. Keep the top portion for your records. - - - - - - - - -

---

| Form **W-4A**
Department of the Treasury
Internal Revenue Service | **Employee's Withholding Allowance Certificate**
▶ For Privacy Act and Paperwork Reduction Act Notice, see reverse. | OMB No. 1545-0010
1987 |

1 Type or print your full name | **2** Your social security number

Home address (number and street or rural route)

City or town, state, and ZIP code

3 Marital Status
☐ Single ☐ Married
☐ Married, but withhold at higher Single rate
Note: *If married, but legally separated, or spouse is a nonresident alien, check the Single box.*

4 Total number of allowances you are claiming (from line G above, or from the Worksheets on back if they apply) . . . | **4** |

5 Additional amount, if any, you want deducted from each pay . . . . | **5** $ |

6 I claim exemption from withholding because (check boxes below that apply):
 a ☐ Last year I did not owe any Federal income tax and had a right to a full refund of **ALL** income tax withheld, **AND**
 b ☐ This year I do not expect to owe any Federal income tax and expect to have a right to a full refund of **ALL** income tax withheld. If both **a** and **b** apply, enter the year effective and "EXEMPT" here . . . . . ▶ | Year 19
 c Are you a full-time student? . . . . ☐ Yes ☐ No

Under penalties of perjury, I certify that I am entitled to the number of withholding allowances claimed on this certificate or, if claiming exemption from withholding, that I am entitled to claim the exempt status.

Employee's signature ▶ _____ **Date** ▶ _____, 1987

7 Employer's name and address (Employer: Complete 7, 8, and 9 only if sending to IRS) | **8** Office code | **9** Employer identification number

FEDERAL UNEMPLOYMENT TAX

File Form 940, *Employer's Annual Federal Unemployment (FUTA) Tax Return*. Also: Form 8109 to make deposits.

The federal unemployment tax system, together with the state systems, provides for payments of unemployment compensation to workers who have lost their jobs. Most employers pay both a state and the federal unemployment tax.

In general you are subject to FUTA tax on the wages you pay employees who are not farm workers or household workers if: (1) in any calendar quarter, the wages you paid to employees in this category totalled $1,500 or more; or (2) in each of 20 different calendar weeks, there was at least a part of a day in which you had an employee in this category. See Circular E for a list of payments excluded from FUTA and a list of types of employment not subject to the tax.

FIGURING THE TAX

The federal unemployment tax is figured on the first $7,000 in wages paid to each employee during 1988. The tax is imposed on you as the employer. You must not collect it or deduct it from the wages of your employees.

TAX RATE

The federal unemployment tax rate is scheduled to be reduced from 6.2% to 6% for 1988. However, you are given a credit of up to 5.4% for the State unemployment tax you pay. The tax rate, therefore, can be as low as 0.6% for 1988 if your state is not subject to a credit reduction. Please note that the 6% for 1988 is not certain and there is legislation being considered to retain the 6.2% FUTA tax rate. Study rules applying to liability for this tax (i.e., credit reduction, success of employer, concurrent employment by related corporations - See Publication 334, Chapter 34).

FORM 940

Employer's Annual Federal Unemployment (FUTA) Tax Return is used for reporting. This form covers one calendar year and is generally due one month after the year ends. However, you may have to make deposits of this tax before filing the return.

DEPOSITS

If at the end of any calendar quarter, you owe but have not yet deposited, more than $100 in Federal unemployment (FUTA) tax for the year, you must make a deposit by the end of the next month.

Due dates are as follows:

If your undeposited FUTA tax is more than $100 on:	Deposit the full amount by
March 31	April 30
June 30	July 31
September 30	October 31
December 31	January 31

If the tax is $100 or less at the end of the quarter, you need not deposit it, but you must add it to the tax for the next quarter and deposit according to the $100 rule. See Publication 334, Chapter 34, *How to Make Deposits*. Use a Federal Tax Deposit Coupon Book containing Form 8109, *Federal Tax Deposit Coupon* to deposit taxes to an authorized financial institution or Federal Reserve Bank.

FORM 8109

Federal Tax Deposit Coupons are used to make deposits to an authorized financial institution or Federal Reserve Bank. You can get the names of authorized institutions from a Federal Reserve Bank. Each deposit must be accompanied by a Federal tax deposit (FTD) coupon. Clearly mark the correct type of tax and tax period on each deposit coupon. The FUTA tax must be deposited separately from the social security and withheld income tax deposits. A federal Tax Deposit Coupon Book containing a supply of Form 8109 coupons and instructions will automatically be sent to you after you apply for an employer identification member.

PUBLICATIONS

(1) Publication 334, *Tax Guide for Small Business*, Chapter 34; (2) Publication 15, *Employer's Tax Guide* (Circular E); (3) Form 940, *FUTA Tax Return* (Instructions); (4) Form 8109, *Federal Tax Deposit Coupon* (instructions); and (5) Publication 539, *Employment Taxes* (discussion under social security taxes).

SAMPLE

The next page shows a sample Form 940, *Employer's Annual Federal Unemployment (FUTA) Tax Return*.

FORM 940

EMPLOYER'S ANNUAL FEDERAL
UNEMPLOYMENT (FUTA) TAX RETURN

Form **940** Department of the Treasury Internal Revenue Service	**Employer's Annual Federal Unemployment (FUTA) Tax Return** ▶ For Paperwork Reduction Act Notice, see page 2.	OMB No. 1545-0028 **1987**

				T
	Name (as distinguished from trade name)		Calendar year	FF
If incorrect, make any necessary change. ▶				FD
	Trade name, if any			FP
				I
	Address and ZIP code		Employer identification number	T
	L		–	

A   Did you pay all required contributions to state unemployment funds by the due date of Form 940? (See instructions if none required.) . . . ☐ **Yes** ☐ **No**

    If you checked the "Yes" box, enter the amount of contributions paid to state unemployment funds . . . . ▶ $ _____

B   Are you required to pay contributions to only one state? . . . . ☐ **Yes** ☐ **No**

    If you checked the "Yes" box: (1) Enter the name of the state where you are required to pay contributions . . . . . . ▶ _____

    (2) Enter your state reporting number(s) as shown on state unemployment tax return. ▶ _____

C   If any part of wages taxable for FUTA tax is exempt from state unemployment tax, check the box. (See the Specific Instructions on page 2.) . . . . ☐

Part I   Computation of Taxable Wages and Credit Reduction (to be completed by all taxpayers)

1	Total payments (including exempt payments) during the calendar year for services of employees	1	
2	Exempt payments. (Explain each exemption shown, attaching additional sheets if necessary.) ▶	Amount paid	
		2	
3	Payments for services of more than $7,000. Enter only the excess over the first $7,000 paid to individual employees not including exempt amounts shown on line 2. Do not use the state wage limitation.	3	
4	Total exempt payments (add lines 2 and 3)	4	
5	**Total taxable wages** (subtract line 4 from line 1). (If any part is exempt from state contributions, see instructions.)▶	5	
6	Additional tax resulting from credit reduction for unpaid advances to the state listed below (by two-letter Postal Service abbreviation). Enter the wages included on line 5 above for that state and multiply by the rate shown. (See the instructions.) Enter the credit reduction amount here and in Part II, line 2, or Part III, line 4: PA _____ x.015= ▶	6	

Part II   Tax Due or Refund (Complete if you checked the "Yes" boxes in both questions A and B and did not check the box in C, above.)

1	FUTA tax. Multiply the wages in Part I, line 5, by .008 and enter here	1	
2	Enter amount from Part I, line 6	2	
3	**Total FUTA tax** (add lines 1 and 2)	3	
4	Minus: Total FUTA tax deposited for the year, including any overpayment applied from a prior year (from your records)	4	
5	**Balance due** (subtract line 4 from line 3). This should be $100 or less. Pay to IRS . . . . . ▶	5	
6	**Overpayment** (subtract line 3 from line 4). Check if it is to be: ☐ Applied to next return, or ☐ Refunded . ▶	6	

Part III   Tax Due or Refund (Complete if you checked the "No" box in either question A or B or you checked the box in C, above. Also complete Part V.)

1	Gross FUTA tax. Multiply the wages in Part I, line 5, by .062	1	
2	Maximum credit. Multiply the wages in Part I, line 5, by .054	2	
3	Enter the smaller of the amount in Part V, line 11, or Part III, line 2	3	
4	Enter amount from Part I, line 6	4	
5	**Credit allowable** (subtract line 4 from line 3). (If zero or less, enter 0.)	5	
6	**Total FUTA tax** (subtract line 5 from line 1)	6	
7	Minus: Total FUTA tax deposited for the year, including any overpayment applied from a prior year (from your records)	7	
8	**Balance due** (subtract line 7 from line 6). This should be $100 or less. Pay to IRS . . . . . ▶	8	
9	**Overpayment** (subtract line 6 from line 7). Check if it is to be: ☐ Applied to next return, or ☐ Refunded . ▶	9	

Part IV   Record of Quarterly Federal Tax Liability for Unemployment Tax (Do not include state liability.)

Quarter	First	Second	Third	Fourth	Total for Year
Liability for quarter					

If you will not have to file returns in the future, write "Final" here (see general instruction "Who Must File") and sign the return. ▶

Under penalties of perjury, I declare that I have examined this return, including accompanying schedules and statements, and to the best of my knowledge and belief, it is true, correct, and complete, and that no part of any payment made to a state unemployment fund claimed as a credit was or is to be deducted from the payments to employees.

Signature ▶   Title (Owner, etc.) ▶   Date ▶

Form **940** (1987)

PAYMENTS TO NON-EMPLOYEES FOR SERVICES RENDERED

File Form 1099-MISC, *Statement for Recipients of Miscellaneous Income.*

If you made payments of $600 or more for fees, commissions, or other forms of compensations to persons not treated as your employees for services rendered in your trade or business, you will have to file Form 1099-MISC. Report payments made in the course of your trade or business, or for which you were a nominee/middleman, or from which you withheld federal income tax or foreign tax.

FORM 1099 MISC

Statement for Recipient of Miscellaneous Income is an information form used to report payments in the course of your trade or business, or for which you were a nominee/middleman, or from which you withheld federal income tax or foreign tax. If payments were in the form of barter, file Form 1099-B.

WHEN AND HOW TO FILE

File 1099-MISC on or before the last day of February. Transmit these forms to IRS with Form 1096, *Annual Summary and Transmittal of U.S. Information Return* . Send Form 1096 and Form 1099-MISC to your IRS Service Center (address in instructions). A copy of the 1099-MISC must be sent to the recipient by January 31st.

PUBLICATIONS

Publication 334, Tax Guide for Small Business, Chapter 37. For more information on 1099's, See Publication 916, *Information Returns* , and *the current year's Instructions* for Forms 1099, 098, 5498, 1096 and W-26.

SAMPLES

The following pages show samples of Form 1099-MISC and 1096.

FORM 1096 (TRANSMITTAL OF U.S. INFORMATION RETURNS)

DO NOT STAPLE 6969 ☐ CORRECTED

| Form **1096**
Department of the Treasury
Internal Revenue Service | **Annual Summary and Transmittal of**
U.S. Information Returns | OMB No. 1545-0108
19**87** |

┌ Type or machine print FILER'S name (or attach label) ┐

    Street address

    City, state, and ZIP code

└   ┘

Paperwork Reduction Act Notice

We ask for this information to carry out the Internal Revenue laws of the United States. We need it to ensure that taxpayers are complying with these laws and to allow us to figure and collect the right amount of tax. You are required to give us this information.

Enter in Box 1 or 2 below the identification number you used as the filer on the attached information returns. Do not fill in both Boxes 1 and 2.

For Official Use Only

| 1 Employer identification number | 2 Social security number | 3 Total number of documents | 4 Federal income tax withheld
$ | 5 Total amount reported with this Form 1096
$ |

Check only one box below to indicate the type of forms attached.

W-2G 32	1098 81	1099-A 80	1099-B 79	1099-DIV 91	1099-G 86	1099-INT 92	1099 MISC 95	1099-OID 96	1099-PATR 97	1099-R 98	5498 28
☐	☐	☐	☐	☐	☐	☐	☐	☐	☐	☐	☐

Under penalties of perjury, I declare that I have examined this return and accompanying documents and, to the best of my knowledge and belief, they are true, correct, and complete. In the case of documents without recipients' identification numbers, I have complied with the requirements of the law in attempting to secure such numbers from the recipients.

Signature ▶ ....   Title ▶ ....   Date ▶ ....

Please return this entire page to the Internal Revenue Service. Photocopies are NOT acceptable.

Instructions

Changes You Should Note.—Form 1096 has been reformatted. Please take care in making entries in the proper boxes. A new Box 5, "Total amount reported with this Form 1096," has been added. No entry is required if you are filing Form 1099-A or 1099-G. For all other forms, enter in Box 5 of Form 1096 the total of the amounts from the specific boxes of the forms listed below:

Form W-2G	Box 1
Form 1098	Box 1
Form 1099-B	Boxes 1b, 2a, 3, and 6
Form 1099-DIV	Boxes 1, 8, and 9
Form 1099-INT	Boxes 1 and 3
Form 1099-MISC	Boxes 1, 2, 3, 5, 6, 7, and 8
Form 1099-OID	Boxes 1 and 2
Form 1099-PATR	Boxes 1, 2, 3, and 5
Form 1099-R	Boxes 1, 8, and 9
Form 5498	Boxes 1 and 2

Purpose of Form.—Use this form to transmit Forms W-2G, 1098, 1099, and 5498 to the Internal Revenue Service.

Completing Form 1096.—If you have received a preprinted label from IRS, place it in the name and address area of the form using the brackets as indicators. Make any necessary corrections to your name and address on the label. However, do not use the label if the taxpayer identification number shown is incorrect. If you are not using a preprinted label, enter the filer's name, address, and taxpayer identification number (TIN) in the spaces provided on the

form. A filer includes a payer, a recipient of mortgage interest payments, a broker, a barter exchange, a trustee or issuer of an individual retirement arrangement (including an IRA or SEP), and a lender who acquires an interest in secured property or who has reason to know that the property has been abandoned. Individuals not in a trade or business should enter their social security number in Box 2; sole proprietors and all others should enter their employer identification number in Box 1. However, sole proprietors who are not required to have an employer identification number should enter their social security number in Box 2.

Group the forms by form number and submit each group with a separate Form 1096. For example, if you must file both Forms 1099-DIV and Forms 1099-INT, complete one Form 1096 to transmit your Forms 1099-DIV and another Form 1096 to transmit your Forms 1099-INT.

In Box 3, enter the number of forms you are transmitting with this Form 1096. Do not include blank or voided forms in your total. Enter the number of correctly completed forms, not the number of pages, being transmitted. For example, if you send one page of three-to-a-page Forms 5498 with a Form 1096 and you have correctly completed two Forms 5498 on that page, enter 2 in Box 3 of Form 1096. Check the appropriate box to indicate the type of form you are transmitting.

If you are filing a Form 1096 for corrected information returns, enter an "X" in the CORRECTED box at the top of this form.

For more information about filing, see the separate Instructions for Forms 1099, 1098, 5498, 1096, and W-2G.

Form **1096** (1987)

Taxes and Recordkeeping

SAMPLE

FORM 1099-MISC (STATEMENT OF RECIPIENTS OF MISC. INCOME)

9595 ☐ VOID ☐ CORRECTED For Official Use Only

Type or machine print PAYER'S name, street address, city, state, and ZIP code	1 Rents $	OMB No. 1545-0115	Miscellaneous Income
	2 Royalties $	19**87** Statement for Recipients of	
PAYER'S Federal identification number / RECIPIENT'S identification number	3 Prizes and awards $	4 Federal income tax withheld $	Copy A For Internal Revenue Service Center
Type or machine print RECIPIENT'S name (first, middle, last)	5 Fishing boat proceeds $	6 Medical and health care payments $	For Paperwork Reduction Act Notice and instructions for completing this form, see Instructions for Forms 1099, 1098, 5498, 1096, and W-2G.
	7 Nonemployee compensation $	8 Substitute payments in lieu of dividends or interest $	
Street address			
City, state, and ZIP code	9 Payer made direct sales of $5,000 or more of consumer products to a buyer (recipient) for resale . . . . . ▶ ☐		
Account number (optional)	10 The amount in Box 7 is crop insurance proceeds · · ▶ ☐		

Form **1099-MISC** Do NOT Cut or Separate Forms on This Page Department of the Treasury - Internal Revenue Service

9595 ☐ VOID ☐ CORRECTED For Official Use Only

Type or machine print PAYER'S name, street address, city, state, and ZIP code	1 Rents $	OMB No. 1545-0115	Miscellaneous Income
	2 Royalties $	19**87** Statement for Recipients of	
PAYER'S Federal identification number / RECIPIENT'S identification number	3 Prizes and awards $	4 Federal income tax withheld $	Copy A For Internal Revenue Service Center
Type or machine print RECIPIENT'S name (first, middle, last)	5 Fishing boat proceeds $	6 Medical and health care payments $	For Paperwork Reduction Act Notice and instructions for completing this form, see Instructions for Forms 1099, 1098, 5498, 1096, and W-2G.
	7 Nonemployee compensation $	8 Substitute payments in lieu of dividends or interest $	
Street address			
City, state, and ZIP code	9 Payer made direct sales of $5,000 or more of consumer products to a buyer (recipient) for resale . . . . . ▶ ☐		
Account number (optional)	10 The amount in Box 7 is crop insurance proceeds · · ▶ ☐		

Form **1099-MISC** Do NOT Cut or Separate Forms on This Page Department of the Treasury - Internal Revenue Service

9595 ☐ VOID ☐ CORRECTED For Official Use Only

Type or machine print PAYER'S name, street address, city, state, and ZIP code	1 Rents $	OMB No. 1545-0115	Miscellaneous Income
	2 Royalties $	19**87** Statement for Recipients of	
PAYER'S Federal identification number / RECIPIENT'S identification number	3 Prizes and awards $	4 Federal income tax withheld $	Copy A For Internal Revenue Service Center
Type or machine print RECIPIENT'S name (first, middle, last)	5 Fishing boat proceeds $	6 Medical and health care payments $	For Paperwork Reduction Act Notice and instructions for completing this form, see Instructions for Forms 1099, 1098, 5498, 1096, and W-2G.
	7 Nonemployee compensation $	8 Substitute payments in lieu of dividends or interest $	
Street address			
City, state, and ZIP code	9 Payer made direct sales of $5,000 or more of consumer products to a buyer (recipient) for resale . . . . . ▶ ☐		
Account number (optional)	10 The amount in Box 7 is crop insurance proceeds · · ▶ ☐		

Form **1099-MISC** Department of the Treasury - Internal Revenue Service

TAXPAYER IDENTIFICATION NUMBER

You generally use your social security number as your taxpayer identification number. You must put this number on each of your individual income tax forms. However, every partnership, S corporation, and corporation must have an employer identification number (EIN) to use as its taxpayer identification number. Sole proprietors must also have EIN's if they pay wages to one or more employees or must file pension or excise tax returns. Otherwise they can use their social security number.

APPLICATION FOR AN EIN

Use Form SS-4, *Application for Employer Identification Number*. These forms are available from Social Security Administration Offices. An SS-5 is used to apply for a Social Security Number Card.

CALENDARS OF FEDERAL TAXES

For your convenience, we have provided tax calendars to serve as a guide in filing the tax returns and information forms discussed above. There is one for each legal structure (sole proprietor, partnership, S corporation, and corporation). It is suggested that you copy the calendar that is appropriate to your business and post it near your recordkeeping area to help remind you to file on the appropriate dates.

It should be noted that these calendars are compiled according to specific dates. **If your tax year is not January 1st through December 31st**, please refer to the footnotes under your calendar. Transpose numbered months into their appropriate months and figure filing dates accordingly.

These calendars will be especially useful combined with your Recordkeeping Schedule which will be presented in the next chapter.

SOLE PROPRIETOR

Calendar Of Federal Taxes For Which You May Be Liable

JANUARY	15	Estimated Tax	Form 1040ES
	31	Social Security (FICA) Tax & Withholding of Income Tax Note: See IRS Rulings for deposit - Pub. 334	941, 941E, 942 & 943
	31	Providing information on Soc. Security (FICA) Tax and the withholding of Income Tax	W-2 (to employee)
	31	Fed. Unemployment (FUTA) Tax	940
	31	Fed. Unemployment (FUTA) Tax (only if liability for unpd. taxes exceeds $100)	8109 (to make deposits)
	31	Information returns to nonemployees and transactions with other persons	Form 1099 (to recipients)
FEBRUARY	28	Information returns to nonemployees and transactions with other persons	Form 1099 (to IRS)
	28	Providing information on soc. security (FICA) Tax and on withholding Income Tax	W-2 & W-3 (to Soc. Sec. Admin.)
APRIL	15	Income Tax	Schedule C (Form 1040)
	15	Self-Employment Tax	Schedule SE (Form 1040)
	15	Estimated Tax	Form 1040ES
	30	Social Security (FICA) Tax & Withholding of Income Tax Note: See IRS Rulings for deposit - Pub. 334	941, 941E, 942 & 943
	30	Federal Unemployment (FUTA) Tax (only if liability for unpd. taxes exceeds $100)	8109 (to make deposits)
JUNE	15	Estimated Tax	Form 1040ES
JULY	31	Social Security (FICA) Tax & Withholding of Income Tax Note: See IRS Rulings for deposit - Pub. 334	941, 941E, 942 & 943
	31	Federal Unemployment (FUTA) Tax (only if liability for unpd. taxes exceeds $100)	8109 (to make deposits)
SEPTEMBER	15	Estimated Tax	Form 1040ES
OCTOBER	31	Social Security (FICA) Tax & Withholding of Income Tax Note: See IRS Rulings for deposit - Pub. 334	941, 941E, 942 & 943
	31	Federal Unemployment (FUTA) Tax (only if liability for unpd. taxes exceeds $100)	8109 (to make deposits)

NOTE: If your tax year is not January 1st thru December 31st--

a. Schedule C (Form 1040) is due the 15th day of the 4th month after the end of the tax year. Schedule SE is due the same day as Form 1040.

b. 1040-ES is due the 15th day of the 4th, 6th, and 9th months of the tax year, and the 15th day of the 1st month after the end of the tax year.

Recordkeeping: The Secret to Growth and Profit

PARTNERSHIP

Calendar of Federal Taxes For Which You May Be Liable

JANUARY	15	Estimated Tax (individual who is a partner)	Form 1040ES
	31	Social Security (FICA) Tax & Withholding of Income Tax Note: See IRS Rulings for deposit - Pub. 334	941, 941E, 942 & 943
	31	Providing information on Soc. Security (FICA) Tax and the withholding of Income Tax	W-2 (to employee)
	31	Fed. Unemployment (FUTA) Tax	940
	31	Fed. Unemployment (FUTA) Tax (only if liability for unpd. taxes exceeds $100)	8109 (to make deposits)
	31	Information returns to nonemployees and transactions with other persons	Form 1099 (to recipients)
FEBRUARY	28	Information returns to nonemployees and transactions with other persons	Form 1099 (to IRS)
	28	Providing information on soc. security (FICA) Tax and on withholding Income Tax	W-2 & W-3 (to Soc. Sec. Admin.)
APRIL	15	Income Tax (Individual who is a partner)	Form 1040
	15	Annual Return of Income	Form 1065
	15	Self-Employment Tax (Indiv. who is partner)	Schedule SE (Form 1040)
	15	Estimated Tax (Individual who is a partner)	Form 1040ES
	30	Social Security (FICA) Tax & Withholding of Income Tax Note: See IRS Rulings for deposit - Pub. 334	941, 941E, 942 & 943
	30	Federal Unemployment (FUTA) Tax (only if liability for unpd. taxes exceeds $100)	8109 (to make deposits)
JUNE	15	Estimated Tax (Individual who is a partner)	Form 1040 ES
JULY	31	Social Security (FICA) Tax & Withholding of Income Tax Note: See IRS Rulings for deposit - Pub. 334	941, 941E, 942 & 943
	31	Federal Unemployment (FUTA) Tax (only if liability for unpd. taxes exceeds $100)	8109 (to make deposits)
SEPTEMBER	15	Estimated Tax (Individual who is a partner)	Form 1040 ES
OCTOBER	31	Social Security (FICA) Tax & Withholding of Income Tax Note: See IRS Rulings for deposit - Pub. 334	941, 941E, 942 & 943
	31	Federal Unemployment (FUTA) Tax (only if liability for unpd. taxes exceeds $100)	8109 (to make deposits)

NOTE: If your tax year is not January 1st thru December 31st--

    a. Income tax due 15th day of 4th mo. after end of tax year.

    b. S-Employment tax due same day as Income Tax (Form 1040).

    c. Estimated Tax (1040ES) is due 15th day of 4th, 6th, and 9th months of tax year and the 15th day of the 1st month after the end of the tax year.

S CORPORATION

Calendar of Federal Taxes For Which You May Be Liable

JANUARY	15	Estimated Tax (Indiv. S Corp. shareholder)	1040ES
	31	Social Security (FICA) Tax & Withholding of Income Tax Note: See IRS Rulings for deposit - Pub. 334	941, 941E, 942 & 943
	31	Providing information on Soc. Security (FICA) Tax and the withholding of Income Tax	W-2 (to employee)
	31	Fed. Unemployment (FUTA) Tax	940
	31	Fed. Unemployment (FUTA) Tax (only if liability for unpd. taxes exceeds $100)	8109 (to make deposits)
	31	Information returns to nonemployees and transactions with other persons	Form 1099 (to recipients)
FEBRUARY	28	Information returns to nonemployees and transactions with other persons	Form 1099 (to IRS)
	28	Providing information on soc. security (FICA) Tax and on withholding Income Tax	W-2 & W-3 (to Soc. Sec. Admin.)
MARCH	15	Income Tax	1120S
APRIL	15	Income Tax (Indiv. S Corp. shareholder)	Form 1040
	15	Estimated Tax (Indiv. S Corp. shareholder)	Form 1040ES
	30	Social Security (FICA) Tax & Withholding of Income Tax Note: See IRS Rulings for deposit - Pub. 334	941, 941E, 942 & 943
	30	Federal Unemployment (FUTA) Tax (only if liability for unpd. taxes exceeds $100)	8109 (to make deposits)
JUNE	15	Estimated Tax (Indiv. S Corp. shareholder)	Form 1040ES
JULY	31	Social Security (FICA) Tax & Withholding of Income Tax Note: See IRS Rulings for deposit - Pub. 334	941, 941E, 942 & 943
	31	Federal Unemployment (FUTA) Tax (only if liability for unpd. taxes exceeds $100)	8109 (to make deposits)
SEPTEMBER	15	Estimated Tax (Indiv. S Corp. shareholder)	Form 1040ES
OCTOBER	31	Social Security (FICA) Tax & Withholding of Income Tax Note: See IRS Rulings for deposit - Pub. 334	941, 941E, 942 & 943
	31	Federal Unemployment (FUTA) Tax (only if liability for unpd. taxes exceeds $100)	8109 (to make deposits)

NOTE: If your tax year is not January 1st thru December 31st--

    a. Schedule C (Form 1040) is due the 15th day of the 4th month after the end of the tax year. Schedule SE is due the same day as Form 1040.

    b. 1040-ES is due the 15th day of the 4th, 6th, and 9th months of the tax year, and the 15th day of the 1st month after the end of the tax year.

CORPORATION

Calendar of Federal Taxes For Which You May Be Liable

JANUARY	31	Social Security (FICA) Tax & Withholding of Income Tax Note: See IRS Rulings for deposit - Pub. 334	941, 941E, 942 & 943
	31	Providing information on Soc. Security (FICA) Tax and the withholding of Income Tax	W-2 (to employee)
	31	Fed. Unemployment (FUTA) Tax	940
	31	Fed. Unemployment (FUTA) Tax (only if liability for unpd. taxes exceeds $100)	8109 (to make deposits)
	31	Information returns to nonemployees and transactions with other persons	Form 1099 (to recipients)
FEBRUARY	28	Information returns to nonemployees and transactions with other persons	Form 1099 (to IRS)
	28	Providing information on soc. security (FICA) Tax and on withholding Income Tax	W-2 & W-3 (to Soc. Sec. Admin.)
MARCH	15	Income Tax	1120 or 1120-A
APRIL	15	Estimated Tax	1120-W
	30	Social Security (FICA) Tax & Withholding of Income Tax Note: See IRS Rulings for deposit - Pub. 334	941, 941E, 942 & 943
	30	Federal Unemployment (FUTA) Tax (only if liability for unpd. taxes exceeds $100)	8109 (to make deposits)
JUNE	15	Estimated Tax	1120-W
JULY	31	Social Security (FICA) Tax & Withholding of Income Tax Note: See IRS Rulings for deposit - Pub. 334	941, 941E, 942 & 943
	31	Federal Unemployment (FUTA) Tax (only if liability for unpd. taxes exceeds $100)	8109 (to make deposits)
SEPTEMBER	15	Estimated Tax	1120-W
OCTOBER	31	Social Security (FICA) Tax & Withholding of Income Tax Note: See IRS Rulings for deposit - Pub. 334	941, 941E, 942 & 943
	31	Federal Unemployment (FUTA) Tax (only if liability for unpd. taxes exceeds $100)	8109 (to make deposits)
DECEMBER	15	Estimated Tax	1120-W

NOTE: If your tax year is not January 1st thru December 31st--

a. Income Tax (Form 1120 or 1120-A) is due the 15th day of the 3rd month after the end of the tax year.

b. Estimated Tax (1120-W) is due the 15th day of the 4th, 6th, 9th, and 12th months of the tax year.

FREE PUBLICATIONS AVAILABLE FROM THE IRS

The following is a list of the publications referred to in the preceding material, along with others which may prove helpful to you in the course of your business. Make it a point to keep a file of tax information. Send for these publications and update your file with new publications at least once a year. The United States Government has spent a great deal of time and money to make this information available to you for preparation of income tax returns.

Information on ordering these publications can be found following this listing. Or if you prefer, you may call IRS toll free at [1 (800) 424-3676].

For a complete listing, see Publication 910, *Guide to Tax Free Services.*
- 334 - *Tax Guide for Small Business*
- 553 - *Highlights of 1987 Tax Changes*
- 910 - *Guide to Free Tax Services*

Begin by reading the three publications listed above. They will give you the most comprehensive information. Others which may be helpful are:
- 15 - *Circular E., Employer's Tax Guide*
- 463 - *Travel, Entertainment & Gift Expenses*
- 505 - *Tax Withholding & Estimated Tax*
- 508 - *Educational Expenses*
- 509 - *Tax Calendars for 1988*
- 533 - *Self-Employment Tax*
- 534 - *Depreciation*
- 535 - *Business Expenses*
- 536 - *Net Operating Losses*
- 538 - *Accounting Periods & Methods*
- 539 - *Employment Taxes*
- 541 - *Taxes on Partnerships*
- 542 - *Tax Information on Corporations*
- 545 - *Deduction for Bad Debts*
- 557 - *Tax-Exempt Status for Your Organization*
- 560 - *Self-Employed Retirement Plans*
- 583 - *Information for Business Taxpayers*
- 587 - *Business Use of Your Hone*
- 589 - *Tax Information on S Corporations*
- 596 - *Earned Income Credit*
- 908 - *Bankruptcy*
- 911 - *Tax Information for Direct Sellers*
- 916 - *Information Returns (Non-employee payments)*
- 917 - *Business Use of a Car*
- 921 - *Explanation of the Tax Reform Act for Business*
- 925 - *Passive Activity & At Risk Rules*

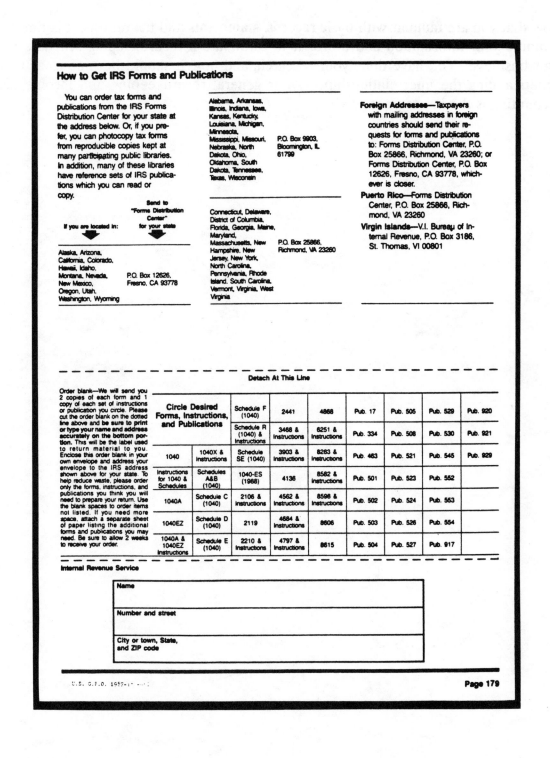

How to Get IRS Forms and Publications

You can order tax forms and publications from the IRS Forms Distribution Center for your state at the address below. Or, if you prefer, you can photocopy tax forms from reproducible copies kept at many participating public libraries. In addition, many of these libraries have reference sets of IRS publications which you can read or copy.

Send to "Forms Distribution Center"

If you are located in: / for your state

Alaska, Arizona, California, Colorado, Hawaii, Idaho, Montana, Nevada, New Mexico, Oregon, Utah, Washington, Wyoming — P.O. Box 12626, Fresno, CA 93778

Alabama, Arkansas, Illinois, Indiana, Iowa, Kansas, Kentucky, Louisiana, Michigan, Minnesota, Mississippi, Missouri, Nebraska, North Dakota, Ohio, Oklahoma, South Dakota, Tennessee, Texas, Wisconsin — P.O. Box 9903, Bloomington, IL 61799

Connecticut, Delaware, District of Columbia, Florida, Georgia, Maine, Maryland, Massachusetts, New Hampshire, New Jersey, New York, North Carolina, Pennsylvania, Rhode Island, South Carolina, Vermont, Virginia, West Virginia — P.O. Box 25866, Richmond, VA 23260

Foreign Addresses—Taxpayers with mailing addresses in foreign countries should send their requests for forms and publications to: Forms Distribution Center, P.O. Box 25866, Richmond, VA 23260; or Forms Distribution Center, P.O. Box 12626, Fresno, CA 93778, whichever is closer.

Puerto Rico—Forms Distribution Center, P.O. Box 25866, Richmond, VA 23260

Virgin Islands—V.I. Bureau of Internal Revenue, P.O. Box 3186, St. Thomas, VI 00801

Detach At This Line

Order blank—We will send you 2 copies of each form and 1 copy of each set of instructions or publication you circle. Please cut the order blank on the dotted line above and be sure to print or type your name and address accurately on the bottom portion. This will be the label used to return material to you. Enclose this order blank in your own envelope and address your envelope to the IRS address shown above for your state. To help reduce waste, please order only the forms, instructions, and publications you think you will need to prepare your return. Use the blank spaces to order items not listed. If you need more space, attach a separate sheet of paper listing the additional forms and publications you may need. Be sure to allow 2 weeks to receive your order.

Circle Desired Forms, Instructions, and Publications

		Schedule F (1040)	2441	4868	Pub. 17	Pub. 505	Pub. 529	Pub. 920
		Schedule R (1040) & Instructions	3468 & Instructions	6251 & Instructions	Pub. 334	Pub. 508	Pub. 530	Pub. 921
1040	1040X & Instructions	Schedule SE (1040)	3903 & Instructions	8283 & Instructions	Pub. 463	Pub. 521	Pub. 545	Pub. 929
Instructions for 1040 & Schedules	Schedules A&B (1040)	1040-ES (1988)	4136	8582 & Instructions	Pub. 501	Pub. 523	Pub. 552	
1040A	Schedule C (1040)	2106 & Instructions	4562 & Instructions	8598 & Instructions	Pub. 502	Pub. 524	Pub. 553	
1040EZ	Schedule D (1040)	2119	4684 & Instructions	8606	Pub. 503	Pub. 526	Pub. 554	
1040A & 1040EZ Instructions	Schedule E (1040)	2210 & Instructions	4797 & Instructions	8615	Pub. 504	Pub. 527	Pub. 917	

Internal Revenue Service

Name
Number and street
City or town, State, and ZIP code

U.S. G.P.O. 1987-1-

Page 179

SUMMARY

The purpose of this chapter has been to introduce you to the tax requirements pertaining to your business. It is important to keep up with and study the revisions that take place in our tax laws. Planning for your business is an ongoing process requiring the implementation of many changes. You may rest assured that many of those changes will be a direct result of new tax laws.

Now that you are familiar with basic records, statements and tax returns, it is time to combine your information and utilize it to formulate a recordkeeping schedule for your business. You have done your research, and now it should become clear that understanding the interrelationship of your general recordkeeping and income tax accounting is the key to your success.

6

RECORDKEEPING SCHEDULES

6. RECORDKEEPING SCHEDULES

If the goal of this book is being reached, you are now the possessor of knowledge in four different, but interrelated areas of recordkeeping. Up to this point, you have been introduced to the following:

BASICS OF RECORDKEEPING

a. Functions and types of recordkeeping
b. When does the recordkeeping begin and who should do it.

ESSENTIAL RECORDS FOR SMALL BUSINESS

a. What are they?
b. Formats

FINANCIAL STATEMENTS DEVELOPED FROM RECORDS

a. Definition of Statement
b. How to develop the Statement
c. What are the information sources for each?

TAXES AND RECORDKEEPING

a. Federal Taxes for which you may be liable
b.   Forms to be used for reporting
c. Publications available as tax aids

All of the above-mentioned information is of no value unless you can organize it into a usable program for doing your recordkeeping. A business owner may feasibly have a wealth of information about his or her particular industry, but failure to utilize that information at the right place and time can lead to business failure. To cite an example, let us assume that you are the seller of a product. You know what the customers want, you have anticipated volume sales, and you have a sufficient stock of your product to meet those needs. If you fail to time your advertising for maximum cost-effectiveness, however, your product will go unsold. Customers' tastes may change, and it can sit on the shelf forever--a useless waste due to a lack of organization.

ORGANIZING YOUR RECORDKEEPING

Just as timing is important to all other phases of your business, it also is important when you deal with Recordkeeping. You cannot haphazardly throw all of your paperwork into a basket and deal with it in a sporadic nature. You will have to organize your Recordkeeping into a system that will allow you to proceed through the tax year in an orderly fashion. That system will have to provide for retrieval and verification of tax information and, at the same time, form a picture of your business that will help you to analyze trends and implement changes to make your venture grow and become more profitable.

BUILDING YOUR SYSTEM

The information in this book was presented in a particular order for a specific reason. Just as a homebuilder must first lay the foundation, do the framing, put up the walls, and then do the finish work, you, too, must build your foundation first and learn the Basics of Recordkeeping. The frame can be likened to Essential Records. It is the underlying material without which there could be no walls. In the same way, Essential Records are the basis for forming Financial Statements. At last, the builder finishes the home and makes some rooms into a limited space for each family member, and other rooms into common areas where the whole family will meet. This is Tax Accounting, with different legal structures functioning within their limited areas, but meeting in areas common to all businesses. The house is complete--and so is your Recordkeeping. Now a schedule needs to be made to maintain your home or it will soon be a shambles. To keep your business in a maintained state, it too must have order. It is time to organize and set up a Recordkeeping Schedule.

Proceeding on the assumption that you have never done Recordkeeping and that you have no idea in what order it must be done, it will be the goal of this section to give you a basic format to follow while you learn this task.

There is a specific order to Recordkeeping, and you must follow that order if your records are going to be effective. Since the two goals of Recordkeeping are retrieval for tax purposes and the analyzing of information for internal planning, your schedule will have to provide for the reaching of those goals.

The following General Recordkeeping Schedule will do just that if you will follow it. Do not fail to do any of the tasks, and be sure to do them on time. POST your schedule on the wall in your office and refer to it every day for what needs to be done. Before long those chores will become automatic. All of the information presented in this book will have assimilated in your mind and you will begin to see the overall picture. At the end of the year, if you have followed the schedule, you will have every piece of financial information at your fingertips. It can be done--and you can do it!

SCHEDULE FORMAT

The General Recordkeeping Schedule is divided into tasks according to frequency. There are six basic divisions -- **DAILY, WEEKLY, MONTHLY, QUARTERLY, ANNUALLY,** and **END OF YEAR.** Each business has its individual needs, and you may have to shift the frequency of some tasks. To begin with, however, follow this progression and it will cover your needs.

Since some tasks are different for different legal structures (i.e., - sole proprietorship, partnership, S corporation, and corporation), it will be noted as to which apply. If there is no notation accompanying the task, it applies to all legal structures.

Keep in mind when you are using the General Recordkeeping Schedule that all the items on the schedule have been covered in one of the previous sections. You need only refer back to the appropriate record, statement, or tax return information to refresh your memory and complete your task. Be sure to keep reference materials mentioned in those sections close at hand in case you need more detailed information.

The next four pages contain a General Recordkeeping Schedule. Copy and Post!

GENERAL RECORDKEEPING SCHEDULE

DAILY

1. File mail in appropriate folders.
2. Unpack and put away incoming inventory.
3. Record inventory information.
4. Pay any invoices necessary to meet discount deadlines.

WEEKLY

1. Prepare income deposit.
2. Enter deposit in Checkbook and General Journal.
3. Enter sales information in Inventory Record.
4. Enter week's checking transactions in General Journal.
5. Record Petty Cash purchases and file receipts.
6. Pay invoices due. Be aware of discount dates.
7. Enter other purchases in appropriate records (ex: tools, office equipment).

MONTHLY

1. Balance checkbook (reconcile with statement).
2. Post information to General Ledger Accounts.
3. Enter any interest earned and any bank charges in General Journal and Checkbook.
4. Total and Balance all journal columns.
5. Total and Balance accounts in ledger.
6. Enter monthly income and expense totals on Profit and Loss Statement.
7. Check Accounts Payable and send out Statements to open accounts.
8. Prepare monthly Income Statement and Balance Sheet.

QUARTERLY

1. File estimated Taxes with the Internal Revenue Service(and with your State, if applicable).

   a. Sole proprietor, individual who is a partner or S corporation shareholder file on 15th day of 4th, 6th, and 9th months of tax year, and 15th day of 1st month after the end of tax year.

   b. Corporations file the 15th day of 4th, 6th, 9th and 12th months of the tax year.

   Note: Only two months lapse between 1st and 2nd quarter filing.

2. File Employers' Quarterly Federal Tax Returns reporting social security (FICA) tax and the withholding of income tax. Check early to see if you are required to make deposits.

3. Make Federal Unemployment (FUTA) tax deposits. Make deposits on 4-30, 7-31, 10-31, and 1-31, but only if the liability for unpaid tax is more than $100.

4. Fill out and send in your sales tax report to the State Board of Equalization (with a check for monies collected for sales tax during the previous quarter). This is for those holding a Seller's Permit. It is not covered in this book (see Chapter 9 in our business start-up book Out of Your Mind...and Into the Marketplace™. Report forms are furnished by the SBE and are due 1/31, 4/31, 7/31 and 10/31 for the previous quarter. If you are only required to file annually, it will be due 1/31 for the previous calendar year.

5. Fill out your quarterly Budget Analysis and adjust budget amounts for the next quarter (i.e. - if you are over, cut controllable expenses in next quarter budget).

ANNUALLY

1. Provide information on social security (FICA) tax and the withholding of income tax.

   a. W-2 to employees on January 31st.
   b. W-2 and W-3 to Social Security Administration on the last day of February.

2. Send Information for payments to nonemployees and transactions with other persons.

   a. Forms 1099 to recipient by 1-31.
   b. Forms 1099 and transmittals 1096 to IRS by 2-28.

3. File Federal unemployment (FUTA) tax returns with the IRS, Due date is 1-31.

4. File Income Tax Returns with the IRS. (State, if applicable)

   a. Sole Proprietor and Individual who is a partner or S Corporation shareholder file on 15th day of the 4th month after end of tax year.
   b. Partnership returns due on the 15th day of 4th month after end of tax year.
   c. S corporations and corporations file on the 15th day of the 3rd month after the end of the tax year.

5. File Self-Employment Tax Return

   a. For sole proprietors or individuals who are partners.
   b. File on the 15th day of 4th month after the end of the tax year (same day and with Form 1040).

END OF TAX YEAR

1. Pay all invoices, sales taxes and other expenses which you wish to use as deductions for the preceding tax year.

2. Transfer 12th month totals from General Journal and Ledger accounts to Profit and Loss Statement.

3. Total Horizontal Columns of Profit and Loss Statement (also known as Income Statement).

4. Prepare a balance Sheet for your business. Monthly Balance Sheets are optional, but you should prepare one at least once a year.

5. Use information from the past year's Profit and Loss Statement to help you do a Pro Forma Cash Flow Statement for the coming year (this is your new Budget).

6. File your sales tax return with the State Board of Equalization.

7. Set up your records for the coming year. Begin your recordkeeping in the first week. Do not get behind. Note, it is a good idea to buy new ledgers and files early, before the supply runs out.

PREPARING FOR
UNCLE SAM

7. PREPARING FOR UNCLE SAM

This book would not be complete without giving you information on preparing your income tax. As was stated earlier, one of the two main purposes of recordkeeping is for income tax retrieval and verification. When all your end-of-the-year work has been done, it is time to begin work on income taxes. By no means am I suggesting that you do it all yourself. As a matter of fact, it is strongly suggested that you hire an accountant to do the final preparation and aid you in maximizing your tax benefits. Not very many of us are well enough informed to have a good command of all the tax regulations and changes. However, you can do a great deal of the preliminary work. This will be of benefit to you in two different ways. **(1) You will save on accounting fees; and (2) You will learn much about your business by working on your taxes.**

There will be a great deal of variation in what you can do yourself, due not only to the complexity of your particular business, but also to the abilities of the individual doing your recordkeeping. For this reason, I will not attempt to give directions for preliminary tax preparations. The only sound advice, at this point, is to tell you to select the tax forms that you will be required to be filled out. Refer to the publications explaining those forms and showing samples of ones that are be filled out. You do have all the information for retrieval and it would be beneficial if you could pull the information needed on the forms from your records and statements and list it for your accountant. Then when you meet with him, you will have the information he needs to complete your returns.

1. List Schedule C, Part II, deductions and compute the total amount for each. I get this information from my Profit and Loss Statement. Note that the Miscellaneous Column must be divided into types of expenses and credited to the proper deduction. Petty cash expenses must be categorized and included in these expenses.

2.

I compute Gross Income (Schedule C, Part I) by retrieving figures from my Profit and Loss Statement. Number 2 in Part I calls for Cost of Goods Sold and/or Operations.

3.

Cost of Goods Sold and/or Operations is determined by completing Schedule C, Part III. This requires an Inventory count. I total my Inventory as of December 31st (Ending Inventory). The beginning Inventory is last year's Ending Inventory. I keep my inventory up-to-date, so this is no big problem. With these figures and information from the Profit & Loss Statement, it is a simple matter to complete Part III and determine the Cost of Goods Sold

4. and/or Operations figure.

I transfer the above figure to Schedule C, Part I and now can complete that section to determine Gross Income.

5.

At this point, I am ready for the accountant. I give him my list of deductions and the figures for completing Gross Income. All he has to do is plug the figures into Parts I, II, and III of Schedule C and figure the depreciation (Part IV). It is then a simple matter for him to arrive at my net profit or loss before taxes.

6. The accountant then does my Form 1040, adds business income and figures the taxes due or refundable. He is the preparer of my tax return and as such takes responsibility for its being correctly done. I pay a small fee and have the comfort of knowing that I have a professional to help maximize my tax benefits, give advice and go to audit with me should the occasion arise.

Some of the things I do before meeting with my accountant are as follows:

All of the above is usually completed by the middle of January. I can now forget about it and go about the business of getting on with the new year.

THE LAST CHORE

The IRS requires us to keep all pertinent information for a period of five years. During that time, our past returns are subject to audit. I have found that it is very effective to file all of the information for one year together. Put the following in a file, mark it with the year, date, and file it away.

1. Income Tax Returns
2. All Receipts
3. Bank Statements
4. General Journal
5. Petty Cash Record
6. Miscellaneous Records and Statements
7. All information pertinent to the verification of that year's returns.

A Records Retention Schedule has been included here for your convenience. Be aware that several records are retained for a period determined by administrative decision. It is a good idea to keep many of the records for the life of your business. Remember that the other purpose of records is that of analyzing trends and implementing changes. They are only useful if they are still in your possession.

RECORDS RETENTION SCHEDULE

RETENTION PERIOD	AUTHORITY TO DISPOSE
1-10 – No. Years to be Retained **PR** – Retain Permanently **EOY** – Retain Until End of Year **CJ** – Retain Until Completion of Job **EXP** – Retain Until Expiration **ED** – Retain Until Equipment Disposal	**AD** – Administrative Decision **FLSA** – Fair Labor Standards Act **CFR** – Code of Federal Regulations **IR** – Insurance Regulation

TYPE OF RECORD	RETAIN FOR	BY WHOSE AUTHORITY
BANK DEPOSIT RECORDS	7	AD
BANK STATEMENTS	7	AD
BUSINESS LICENSES	EXP	AD
CATALOGS	EXP	AD
CHECK REGISTER	PR	AD
CHECKS (CANCELLED)	3	FLSA, STATE
CONTRACTS	EXP	AD
CORRESPONDENCE	5	AD
DEPRECIATION RECORDS	PR	CFR
ESTIMATED TAX RECORDS	PR	AD
EXPENSE RECORDS	7	AD
INSURANCE (CLAIMS RECORDS)	11	IR
INSURANCE POLICIES	EXP	AD
INVENTORY RECORD	10	AD
INVENTORY REPORTS	PR	CFR
INVOICES (ACCT. PAYABLE)	3	FLSA, STATE
INVOICES (ACCT. RECEIVABLE)	7	AD
LEDGER (GENERAL)	PR	CFR
MAINTENANCE RECORDS	ED	AD
OFFICE EQUIPMENT RECORDS	5	AD
PATENTS	PR	AD
PETTY CASH RECORD	PR	AD
POSTAL RECORDS	1	AD, CFR
PURCHASE ORDERS	3	CFR
SALES TAX REPORTS TO STATE	PR	STATE
SHIPPING DOCUMENTS	2-10	AD, CFR
TAX BILLS & STATEMENTS	PR	AD
TAX RETURNS (FED. & STATE)	PR	AD
TRADEMARKS & COPYRIGHTS	PR	AD
TRAVEL RECORDS	7	AD
WORK PAPERS (PROJECTS)	CJ	AD
YEAR-END REPORTS	PR	AD

ANALYZING
FINANCIAL STATEMENTS

written by:

MARILYN J. DAUBER, C . P . A .

Marilyn J. Dauber is a C.P.A. in Butte, Montana. Her success at helping businesses that are in trouble has been greatly enhanced by her ability to analyze financial statements and implement the appropriate changes. We would like to thank her for sharing her expertise with us through the contribution of this chapter. Because of her generosity, the user of this book has the opportunity not only to set up and maintain the proper records, but to gain the maximum benefits from those records through financial statement analysis.

8. ANALYZING FINANCIAL STATEMENTS

FINANCIAL STATEMENTS

Your financial statements contain the information **you** need to help make decisions regarding **your** business. Many small business owners think of their financial statements as requirements for creditors, bankers, or tax preparers only, but they are much more than that. When analyzed, your financial statements can give you the key information you need on the financial condition and the operations of your business.

Financial statement analysis requires measures to be expressed as ratios or percentages. For example, consider the situation where total assets on your balance sheet are $10,000.00. Cash is $2,000; Accounts Receivable are $3,000; and Fixed Assets are $5,000. The relationships would be expressed as follows:

	Ratio	Ratio Relationship	Percentages
Cash	.2	.2:1	20%
Accounts Receivable	.3	.3:1	30%
Fixed Assets	.5	.5:1	50%

Financial statement analysis involves the studying of relationships and comparisons of items (1) in a single year's financial statement, (2) comparative financial statements for a period of time, and (3) with other businesses.

Many analytic tools are available, but we will focus on the following measures that are of most importance to a small business owner:

> Liquidity Analysis
> Profitability Analysis
> Measures of Debit
> Measures of Investment
> Vertical Financial Statement Analysis
> Horizontal Financial Statement Analysis

Let's take a look ,on the few pages, at some ratios that may help you to evaluate your business. To illustrate, we will use the following statements from a small business, we will call it Mary's Flower Shop.

Mary's Flower Shop
Comparative Balance Sheet
12/31/87 and 12/31/86

	1987	1986
Assets		
Current Assets:		
Cash	$ 2,000	$ 5,000
Accounts Receivable	3,000	1,000
Inventory	$ 5,000	3,000
Total Current Assets	$10,000	$ 9,000
Fixed Assets	8,000	5,000
Total Assets	$18,000	$14,000
Liabilities & Owner's Equity		
Current Liabilities		
Accounts Payable	$ 4,000	$ 2,000
Taxes Payable	220	300
Total Current Liabilities	$ 4,220	$ 2,300
Long Term Liabilities	10,000	8,000
Total Liabilities	$14,220	$10,300
Owner's Equity	3,780	3,700
Total Liabilities & Owner's Equity	$18,000	$14,000

Mary's Flower Shop
Comparative Income Statement
For years ended 12/31/87 and 12/31/86

	1987	1986
Sales	$ 8,000	$ 6,000
Cost of Goods Sold	6,000	3,900
Gross Profit	$ 2,000	$ 2,100
Direct Expenses:		
Advertising	$ 100	$ 50
Freight	50	40
Salaries	$ 150	$ 150
Total Direct Expenses	$ 300	$ 240
Indirect Expenses:		
Rent	$ 450	$ 250
Insurance	150	125
Utilities	150	100
Total Indirect Expenses	$ 750	$ 475
Income from Operations	$ 950	$ 1,385
Interest Expense	720	450
Taxes	150	180
Net Profit <Loss>	$ 80	$ 755

LIQUIDITY ANALYSIS

The liquidity of a business is the ability it has to meet financial obligations. The analysis focuses on the balance sheet relationships for the current assets and current liabilities.

NET WORKING CAPITAL

The excess of current assets over current liabilities is net working capital. The more net working capital a business has, the less risky it is, as it has the ability to cover current liabilities as they come due. Let's take a look at the net working capital for Mary's Flower Shop:

	1987	1986
Current Assets	$10,000	$ 9,000
Current Liabilities	4,220	2,300
Net Working Capital	5,780	6,700

In both years, net working capital was present, which would indicate a good position. But let's analyze this a bit more to get a clear picture of the liquidity of Mary's Flower Shop.

CURRENT RATIO

The current ratio is a more dependable indication of liquidity than the net working capital. The current ratio is computed with the following formula:

$$\text{Current Ratio} = \frac{\text{Current Assets}}{\text{Current Liabilities}}$$

For Mary's Flower Shop, the current ratios are:

1987: $\dfrac{\$10,000}{\$ 4,220} = 2.37$

1986: $\dfrac{\$ 9,000}{\$ 2,300} = 3.91$

As you can see, the business was in a more liquid position in 1986. In 1987, the business did experience an increase in current assets, but it also had a increase in current liabilities.

There is no set criteria for the **normal** current ratio, as that is dependent on the business you are in. If you have predictable cash flows, you can operate with a lower current ratio.

The ratio of 2.0 is considered acceptable for most businesses. A ratio of 2.0 would allow a company to lose 50% of its current assets and still be able to cover current liabilities. For most businesses, this is an adequate margin of safety.

For Mary's Flower Shop, the **decrease** in the current ratio would cause the owner to investigate further.

QUICK RATIO

Since inventory is the most difficult current asset to dispose of quickly, it is subtracted from the current assets in the quick ratio to give a tougher list of liquidity. The quick ratio is computed as follows:

$$\text{Quick Ratio} = \frac{\underline{\text{Current Assets - Inventory}}}{\text{Current Liabilities}}$$

The quick Ratios for our case are:

$$1987: \quad \frac{\$10,000 - 5,000}{\$4,220} = 1.18$$

$$1986: \quad \frac{\$9,000 - 3,000}{\$2,300} = 2.61$$

A quick ratio of 1.00 or greater is usually recommended, but that is dependent upon the business you are in.

From the analysis of the liquidity measures (net working capital, current ratio and quick ratio), we see that the 1987 results are within acceptable limits. The business did experience a decrease in liquidity, and is viewed as more risky than in 1986.

You can use these ratios to see if your business is in any risk of insolvency. You will also be able to assess your ability to increase or decrease current assets for your business strategy. How would these moves affect your liquidity?

Your creditors will use these ratios to determine whether or not to extend credit to you. They will compare the ratios for previous periods and with those of similar businesses.

PROFITABILITY ANALYSIS

Profitability analysis will measure the ability of a business to make a profit.

GROSS PROFIT MARGIN

The gross profit margin indicates the percentage of each sales dollar remaining after a business has paid for its goods.

$$\text{Gross Profit Margin} = \frac{\underline{\text{Gross Profit}}}{\text{Sales}}$$

The higher the gross profit margin, the better. For Mary's Flower Shop, the gross profit margins were:

$$1987: \quad \frac{\$2,000}{\$8,000} \quad = \quad 25\%$$

$$1986: \quad \frac{\$2,100}{\$6,000} = \quad 35\%$$

The **normal** rate is dependent on the business you are in. The Gross Profit Margin is the actual mark-up you have on the goods sold. In 1987, our case has a 25% contribution margin which means that 25 cents of every dollar in sales is left to cover the direct, indirect, and other expenses. Mary's Flower Shop can be viewed as "less profitable" in 1987 as compared to 1986.

OPERATING PROFIT MARGIN

This ratio represents the **pure** operations profits, ignoring interest and taxes. A high operating profit margin is preferred.

$$\textbf{Operating Profit Margin} = \frac{\textbf{Income from Operations}}{\textbf{Sales}}$$

Mary's Flower Shop has the following ratios:

$$1987: \quad \frac{\$\ 950}{\$8,000} = \quad 11.88\%$$

$$1986: \quad \frac{\$1,385}{\$6,000} = \quad 23.08\%$$

Again our case is showing a less profitable position in 1987.

NET PROFIT MARGIN

The net profit margin is clearly the measure of a business' success with respect to earnings on sales.

$$\textbf{Net Profit Margin} \quad = \quad \frac{\textbf{Net Profit}}{\textbf{Sales}}$$

A higher margin means the firm is more profitable. The net profit margin will differ according to your business. A 1% margin for a grocery store is not unusually due to the large quantity of items handled; while a 10% margin for a jewelry store would be considered low.

Mary's Flower Shop has the following net profit margins:

1987: $\dfrac{\$\ \ \ 80}{\$8,000}$ = 1%

1986: $\dfrac{\$\ \ 755}{\$6,000}$ = 12.6%

Clearly, Mary's Flower Shop is in trouble. All the ratios indicate a decrease in profitability from 1986.

As a business owner, you can see just how profitable your business is. If the ratios are too low, you will want to analyze why.

> **Did you mark up your goods sold enough? Check your gross profit margin.**
>
> **Are your operating expenses too high? Check your operating profit margin.**
>
> **Are your interest expenses too high? Check your net profit margin.**

For Mary's Flower shop, all of the above questions can be answered using the ratios we computed.

Your creditors will look at these ratios to see just how profitable your business is. Without profits, a business can't attract outside financing.

DEBT MEASURES

The debt position of a business indicates the amount of other people's money that is being used to generate profits. Many new businesses assume too much debt too soon in an attempt to grow too quickly. The measures of debt will tell a business how indebted it is and how able it is to service the debts. The more indebtedness, the greater the risk of failure.

DEBT RATIO
This is a key financial ratio used by creditors.

Debt Ratio = $\dfrac{\textbf{Total Liabilities}}{\textbf{Total Assets}}$

The higher this ratio, the more risk of failure. For Mary's Flower Shop, the debt ratios are:

$$1987: \qquad \frac{\$14,200}{\$18,000} \qquad = \qquad 79\%$$

$$1986: \qquad \frac{\$10,300}{\$14,000} \qquad = \qquad 74\%$$

The acceptable ratio is dependent upon the policies of your creditors and bankers. The rates of 79% and 74% above are excessively high and show a very high risk of failure. Clearly 3/4 of the company is being financed by others' money, and it does not put the business in a good position for acquiring new debt.

If your business plan includes the addition of long-term debt at a future point, you will want to monitor your debt ratio. Is it within the limits acceptable to your banker?

INVESTMENT MEASURES

As a small business owner, you have invested money to acquire assets, and you should be getting a return on these assets. Even if the owner is taking a salary from the business, he/she also should be earning an additional amount for the **investment** in the company.

RETURN ON INVESTMENT (ROI)

The Return on Investment measures the effectiveness of you as the business owner, to generate profits from the available assets.

$$\text{ROI} \quad = \quad \frac{\textbf{Net Profits}}{\textbf{Total Assets}}$$

The higher the ROI, the better. The business owner should get a target for the ROI. What do you want your investment to earn?

For Mary's Flower Shop, the ROI is as follows:

$$1987: \qquad \frac{\$\ \ 80}{\$18,000} = \qquad .4\%$$

$$1986: \qquad \frac{\$\ \ 755}{\$14,000} = \qquad 5.4\%$$

We do no know Mary's target for ROI, but .4% would seem unacceptable. She could put her money in a savings account and earn 5%, so it doesn't appear that a .4% return on her investment is good.

Many small business owners have successfully created jobs for themselves, but still don't earn a fair return on their investment. Set your target for ROI, and work towards it.

VERTICAL FINANCIAL STATEMENT ANALYSIS

Percentage analysis is used to show the relationship of the components in a single financial statement.

For a balance sheet, each asset is stated as a percent of total assets, and each liability and equity item is stated as a percent of total liabilities and equity.

In vertical analysis of the income statement, each item is stated as a percent of net sales.

Let's do a vertical analysis of the income statements for Mary's Flower Shop as shown on the next page.

From the vertical analysis, we can see the following:

1. The components of cost of goods sold and gross profit showed significant difference.

   The 10% increase in cost of goods sold should alert the owner to investigate. Did the cost of the items really increase 10%? Is there a possibility of theft which caused the variance?

   The 10% decrease in gross profit should trigger the owner to look at the mark-up. Is it too low?

2. The composition of direct expenses changed. The owner would want to evaluate the appropriateness of the increase in adverting and decrease in salaries.

3. The composition of indirect expenses would alert the owner to evaluate the increase in rent. Why did this occur and is it necessary?

4. The increase in interest should be analyzed. Most likely, it is due to increase in debt.

Mary's Flower Shop
Comparative Income Statement
For Years Ended 12/31/87 and 12/31/88

	1987		1986	
	Amount	Percent	Amount	Percent
Sales	$8,000	100%	$6,000	100%
Cost of Goods Sold	6,000	75%	3,900	65%
Gross Profit	$2,000	25%	$2,100	35%
Direct Expenses				
Advertising	$ 100	1.3%	$ 50	.8%
Freight	50	.6%	40	.7%
Salaries	150	1.9%	150	2.5%
Total Direct Expenses	$ 300	3.8%	$ 240	4 %
Indirect Expenses:				
Rent	$ 450	5.6%	$ 250	4.2%
Insurance	150	1.9%	125	2.1%
Utilities	150	1.9%	100	1.7%
Total Direct Expenses	$ 750	9.4%	$ 475	7.9%
Income from Operations	$ 950	11.9%	$1,385	23 %
Interest (Paid)	720	9 %	450	7.5%
Taxes	150	1.9%	180	3 %
Net profit <Loss>	$ 80	1 %	$ 755	12.6%

Mary's Flower Shop
Comparative Income Statement
For Years Ended 12/3187 and 12/31/86

	1987	1986	Increase Amount	<Decrease> Percent
Sales	$8,000	$6,000	$2,000	33.3%
Cost of Goods Sold	6,000	3,900	2,100	53.8%
Gross Profit	$2,000	$2,100	<$100>	<4.8%>
Direct Expenses:				
Advertising	$ 100	$ 50	$ 50	100%
Freight	50	40	10	25%
Salaries	150	150	--	--
Total Direct Expenses	$ 300	$ 240	60	25%
Indirect Expenses:				
Rent	$ 450	$ 250	200	80 %
Insurance	150	125	25	20 %
Utilities	150	100	50	50 %
Total Indirect Expenses	$ 750	$ 475	275	57.9%
Income from Operations	$ 950	$1,385	<435>	<31.4%>
Interest (Paid)	720	450	270	60 %
Taxes	150	180	< 30>	<16.7%>
Net Profit <Loss>	$ 80	$ 755	<675>	<89.4%>

HORIZONTAL FINANCIAL STATEMENT ANALYSIS

Horizontal analysis is a percentage analysis of the increases and decreases in the items on comparative financial statements. The increase or decrease of the item is listed, and the earlier statement is used as the base. The percentage of increase or decrease is listed. On the following page is a horizontal analysis of the income statements for Mary's Flower Shop.

From the horizontal analysis of the financial statements, we should evaluate the following:

1. The 33.3% increase in sales resulted in a 4.8% gross profit. This would alert the owner that something is wrong. Is the mark-up sufficient? Was there an according adjustment?

2. The 100% increase in advertising expense was steep. did this expense increase sales? Was it justified?

3. The 80% rent increase and 50% utilities increase should be looked at. Are they justified?

4. The 60% interest increase is most likely a result of increased debt. The owner would want to analyze the components and decide if the interest level is correct or if some debt should be retired.

5. The 89.4% decrease in net profit is not acceptable, and the owner should reevaluate the business.

SUMMARY

Now, you can see how financial statement analysis can be a tool to help **you** manage your business.

If the analysis produces results that don't meet your expectation or if the business is in danger of failure, you must analyze your expenses and your use of assets. Your first step should be to cut expenses and increase the productivity of your assets.

If your return on investment is too low, examine how you could make your assets (equipment, machinery, fixtures, inventory, etc.) work better for your benefits.

If your profit is low, be sure that your mark up is adequate, analyze your operating expenses to see that they are not to high, and review your interest expenses.

If your liquidity is low, you could have a risk of becoming insolvent. Examine the level and composition of current assets and current liabilities.

The vertical and horizontal financial statement analysis will reveal trends and compositions that signify trouble. Using your management skills, **you** can take corrective action.

SMALL BUSINESS REPORTER
Bank of America
Department 3120
P.O. Box 37000
San Francisco, CA 94137

Request "Publication Index" which lists Small Business Reporter Titles available. There is a small charge for the publications.

"Financing Small Business" SBR-104
"Understanding Financial Statements" SBR-109
"Cash Flow-Cash Management" SBR-112
"Financial Records for Small Business" SBR-128

SUPERINTENDENT OF DOCUMENTS
Government Printing Office
Washington, D.C. 20402

Request order forms for "business development booklets, pamphlets, and management assistance publications."

"Basic Budgets for Profit Planning" MA-1.004
"Accounting Services for Small Service Firms" MA-1.010
"Analyze Your Records to Reduce Costs" MA-1.011
"Keeping Records in a Small Business" MA-1.017

"Handbook of Small Business Finance" No. 5
"Financial Management: How to Make a Go of Your Business" No. 44

U.S. DEPARTMENT OF COMMERCE
Office of Consumer Affairs
Room H5725
Washington, D.C   20230

Request copy of the following publication.

"Credit and Financial Issues"

Foster, A., FINANCIAL STATEMENT ANALYSIS, Prentice-Hall, New Jersey, 1981.

Horngren, Charles, INTRODUCTION TO FINANCIAL ACCOUNTING, Prentice-Hall, Inc., New Jersey, 1981.

A

B

C

D

E

F

G

H

I

J

L

M

N

O

P

Q

Quarterly Budget Analysis, 66,67
Quick Ratio, 141

R

Ratios, 137
Receipt Files, 43
Receipts, 43
Recordkeeping Schedules, 119, 123-127
Records Retention, 134
Retrieval of Information, 132
Return on Investment (ROI), 144, 145

S

Schedule Format, 123
Schedule C (Form 1040), 75, 77-79
Schedule E (Form 1040), 80
Schedule K (Form 1065) 76, 80-82
Schedule SE (Form 1040), 76, 95
Schedule 1040-ES, 88, 90
Self-Employment Tax (Individual who is Partner), 93-95
Self-Employment Tax (Individual who is S corporation shareholder), 93-95
Self-Employment Tax (Sole Proprietor), 93-95
Service Industry, 41
Simplicity is Key, 4
Single Entry, 18
Social Security (FICA) Tax, 96, 97
Social Security Number 93, 109
Social Security Taxes, 93, 96
Sources of Cash Worksheet, 62
Special Retail Sales Business, 41

T

U

V

W

NOTES

NOTES

Small Business Consulting
Textbooks
Seminars

OTHER BOOKS

by

L INDA PINSON & JERRY J INNETT

1. OUT OF YOUR MIND...AND INTO THE MARKETPLACE™

A step-by-step guide for starting and succeeding with a small or home-based business. Takes you through the mechanics of business start-up and provides you with an overview of information on such topics as copyrights, trademarks, and patents, legal structures, financing, and marketing.

2. ANATOMY OF A BUSINESS PLAN

A hands-on format for the user. Will enable you to research and write your own business plan. This book is designed to take away the mystery and help you to put together a plan that will both satisfy a lender and enable you to analyze your company and implement changes that will insure success.

3. MARKETING: RESEARCHING AND REACHING YOUR TARGET MARKET

A comprehensive guide to marketing your business. This book not only shows you how to reach your target market, but gives you a wealth of information on how to research that market through the use of library resources, questionnaires, etc.

These books are available through your bookstore or directly from the publisher, OUT OF YOUR MIND...AND INTO THE MARKETPLACE™.

OUT OF YOUR MIND...AND INTO THE MARKETPLACE™
3031 Colt Way - No. 223 Fullerton, CA 92633
Tel. No. (714) 739-1777